Betsy Lee

AUGSBURG Publishing House • Minneapolis

MIRACLE IN THE MAKING

Library of Congress Catalog Card No. 82-072647

International Standard Book No. 0-8066-1954-6

Scripture quotations unless otherwise noted are from the Revised Standard Version of the Bible, copyright 1946, 1952, and 1971 by the Division of Christian Education of the National Council of Churches.

Scripture quotations marked NIV are from the Holy Bible: New International Version. Copyright 1978 by the New York International Bible Society. Used by permission of Zondervan Bible Publishers.

Scripture quotations marked NASB are from the New American Standard Bible, © 1960, 1962, 1963, 1968, 1971, 1972, 1973 by The Lockman Foundation.

Scripture quotations marked KJV are from the Holy Bible: King James Version.

Photos: RNS, 16; Robert J. Cunningham, 35; Darlene Pfister, 43, 49, 98; Bob Taylor, 55; James Schaffer, 69; Jerry Bushey, 76; Willie L. Hill Jr., 83; Mike Burkey, 89; Ron Meyer, 105; Steve Takatsuno, 119.

MANUFACTURED IN THE UNITED STATES OF AMERICA

To exist is to be a child of God
And to know it,
    to feel it,
Is to rejoice forevermore.

George Macdonald

For my mother and father,
who set me going God's way

Contents

Preface

She was at it again, running through the grocery store, snatching cans off the shelf, causing chaos. "Brenna, *no!*"

"Is that your little girl?" an old man asked.

"Yes," I replied, shrugging my shoulders in dismay.

"Ah," he smiled, ". . . a gift from God."

That simple statement shocked me. Of course I knew that my daughter was a gift from God—I had just written a book on that very subject! But how often we forget.

As new parents we fall head over heels in love with our babies. "It's such a miracle," we whisper, gazing at their tiny toes and fingers. New life inspires wonder; we are awestruck, at a loss for words.

Gradually everyday demands of child rearing take over. It is easy to lose sight of the miraculous. In the grocery store that day I was filled with anger and frustration, and a stranger had to remind me how precious my daughter was.

May this book be a reminder to you and to me that our children are God-given and that the wonder we feel as new parents is meant to continue and grow. The miracle of new life doesn't stop at the moment of birth; it is a creative experience that unfolds day by day, drawing us closer to each other and to God.

When I became a parent, it dawned on me that God was going to speak to me through motherhood. This shouldn't have surprised me. God reveals himself through immediate, down-to-earth experiences that are common to us all.

The love between parent and child is a basic human experience, but for a Christian that special relationship has added significance. While we are mothers and fathers giving love as parents, we are also children of God receiving love from our heavenly Father. Understanding the parallels between the two relationships strengthened my faith and increased my joy as a parent.

In this book I want to share my insights with you, exploring our role as Christian parents and our role as children of God. What does parenthood teach us about the nature of God the Father? How does his love equip us to become better parents to our own children?

This is the personal story of how my husband and I grew closer to each other and to God through the gift of our baby. The first chapter describes how we grappled with the decision to have a child. The following chapters focus on each phase of the parent-child relationship as it evolves, from the first ecstatic moment when we fall in love with our newborn to the more difficult times when we have to learn to live with a willful toddler.

These are only the opening chapters of the story—our miracle is still in the making. Brenna is teaching us something new about human and heavenly love every day.

My prayer is that you too will grow in God's love through the gift of your baby and discover all that God wants you to be as parents and believers. I wish you well in the making of *your* miracle.

1

A Time Together

Choosing parenthood

When I called the Malt Shop to make reservations, I asked the waitress for a particular table. It was a special occasion. "Oh," she said, as if she knew, "you want the table for two in the corner." I laughed. She must have thought I meant a romantic occasion, perhaps the beginning of a love affair. In a way I *was* celebrating a love affair. Not with a tall, dark, handsome man, though he would be there. No, the object of my affection was a pixy with sparkling eyes—my baby.

A year before, my husband, Larry, and I had been sipping shakes at the Malt Shop when I felt the birth pangs begin. It seemed a fitting place to celebrate my daughter's first birthday. Brenna sat in her high chair, bubbling with excitement, as her father and I sang "Happy Birthday." She applauded herself, then she balanced a cardboard box on her head, entertaining everyone in the restaurant.

Larry and I never guessed that this engaging little person could change our lives so dramatically. As I watched Brenna smear chocolate cake on her face and grin for Larry's camera, the opposite poles of my life, the past and present, seemed to collide.

Around me slender waitresses in beads and flouncy hats danced between the tables. They reminded me of my carefree college days. As conversation hummed in the restaurant, a guitar player strummed a tune I had heard often in the '60s: "I am a rock. I am an island. And a rock feels no pain; and an island never cries."

The words of that song sounded foreign to me. I was no longer a barefoot, breezy girl, self-sufficient, beholden to no one. I was the mother of a one-year-old. I felt pain, and I cried often, but I also experienced profound joy and laughed with greater abandon. I felt more alive than I had ever been, and I was more in love.

Larry showed Brenna how to pucker her lips and blow out the candle on her cake. "Puff!" A tiny stream of smoke wafted upward, followed by more applause, more laughter. Suddenly I saw a vision of the future without Brenna. What if we had decided not to have a baby? What if her laughter had never lit up our lives?

It had not been an easy decision to become parents. Larry and I were blessed with boundless opportunities: professional ambition, travel, busy lives. Why should we choose to burden ourselves with a child? I had to sift through a mountain of misconceptions and doubts before I came to terms with motherhood.

When I got married, the prospect of having children had only vaguely crossed my mind. I would probably have a family one day, but that day seemed far in the future. I had not given it much thought, one way or the other. Suddenly I was 29. People said, "You should start your family by the time you are 30."

Panic set in. Me—a mother? I couldn't imagine myself waking up bleary-eyed at midnight or washing four dozen diapers a week. Becoming a mother would mean a drastic change in my life-style, adapting my career plans. . . . Could I do it? Why should I feel obligated to try?

Making the choice whether or not to have children was an awesome responsibility. I couldn't make the decision casually or half-heartedly, just to please my parents or friends. I had to decide for myself based on reasons that made sense to me. For the next year, I searched for answers to the question, "Why have children?"

There were the traditional reasons. Children are so much fun! They'll keep you young! You can bounce them on your knee, cuddle them, and buy them toys. And you won't have to face growing old alone.

Kids are a handful, said the mother of terrifying toddlers as she picked up the pieces of a shattered ashtray, but they teach you tolerance, flexibility, and resilience. They stretch you (like a rubber band!).

If you believe in bettering the world, argued a philosophical father, you must have children to pass on your moral values and ideals. They can be a positive force for good.

On the other side of the argument, there were the popular reasons not to have children. Why bring a child into a world torn by war and strife? Do you want to contribute to the population explosion? Well, no, I thought. Perhaps I should adopt, subtracting from the world's problems rather than adding to them.

A child, whether biological or adopted, is certainly going to change your life-style, said my childless friends with carefree schedules. "Joe is taking me out to dinner every night this week," said Kim, who was expecting soon. "There won't be time when the baby comes."

11

If I chose motherhood, it seemed that my life would no longer be my own. There would be countless demands on my time, tears to kiss away, broken bones to mend. . . . Yet parents assured me, "You will be willing to give your children more than you have given anyone or anything before. In the giving you will find real meaning to your life."

This, of course, is the paradox of love: the more you give, the more you receive. Everyone wants to be loved. Who can resist the open affection of a child—so simple, so unconditional, so freely given? Ask the question, "Do you have any children?" and watch a father's beaming face as he shows you the photographs in his wallet.

The love of a child is so appealing that many people become parents for the wrong reason. Couples who have lost their love for one another sometimes hope that a child will bring them back together. Sadly, the added burden often causes conflict rather than harmony.

Larry and I agreed that children should be the result of real love, not a substitute for it. Were we ready to become parents? During the first five years of our marriage, I would have said no. We knew we had a lot of growing up to do ourselves before we nourished the growth of a child. To provide a firm foundation for a family, our hearts and minds had to be truly united. This common commitment had been missing from our marriage.

Even during our courtship, we were at odds. I was 20 and Larry was 22 when we met and fell in love. Four turbulent years passed before we finally decided to get married. I loved Larry, but I didn't want to surrender my independence. He loved me, but the financial burden and responsibilities of marriage frightened him. Our career plans seemed to lead in separate directions.

Still, we wanted to be together. We knew that marriage

called for sacrifice, give and take, putting the other person first. We trusted that God would make our love for one another grow so that this would be possible. Marriage, we concluded, was an act of faith.

We were married in a candlelight ceremony on New Year's Eve. Before our vows were exchanged, we recited a passage from Kahlil Gibran's *The Prophet* (Alfred A. Knopf, 1969), a popular favorite of college couples at the time:

Give your hearts, but not into
   each other's keeping.
For only the hand of Life
   can contain your hearts.
And stand together yet not too near together:
For the pillars of the temple stand apart,
And the oak tree and the cypress grow not
   in each other's shadow.

Not too near together. Even as we swore to become one in marriage, we clung stubbornly to our independence. It was not easy to put aside old patterns, to shed selfishness for selflessness.

After we were married, we packed our trunks and moved to England. Larry had won a scholarship to study at Sheffield University. He attended classes while I basked in English literature and wrote poetry. It was a dreamlike existence.

The dream ended when Larry graduated and we were no longer supported by his scholarship. We both went to work. I was forced to abandon my literary aspirations to write public relations copy, which I resented. Larry pleaded for me to be practical; I accused him of killing something dear to me. Our honeymoon was over.

Christian marriages may be made in heaven, but they have

to be maintained on earth. We had lost the common vision of God's plan for our lives and his provision for us to be help-mates, supporting one another and sharing our concerns openly. Once that bond was broken, we began to drift dangerously apart.

It didn't take long for communication to break down. Our conversations ended in arguments and accusations. I raved and Larry retreated in silence. Finally we stopped talking altogether. We became absorbed in our jobs, spending more time at work than we did together.

Where was God in all of this? Grieving, I'm sure. We had banished him from our relationship. We no longer prayed together or shared the joy of worship and fellowship of other Christians.

A friend of mine confided that her marriage was rocky too. She and her husband lived in an isolated cottage far from their Christian friends in London and an ocean away from a Christian community that had nurtured them in the United States. Without that support, their faith had lost its meaning, and they felt alienated from one another and from God. I knew exactly what she meant.

That year Larry and I flew home on separate vacations to see our parents. Although we did not let them know that our relationship was strained, I'm sure they guessed that something was wrong.

Going home for me was a time of renewal, reuniting with loved ones, discovering parts of me that I had left behind. I had a compelling urge to reread the old love letters that Larry had sent me during our engagement. Had we really loved each other once? What were we like then?

Larry's letters were filled with tenderness and longing. He'd even written poetry! I tried to fight back the tears as I read, "I need you. I want you. I love you." He had not used those words since the early days of our marriage. Neither had I.

What had happened to us? We both cherished marriage as a sacred covenant that would last forever. Now, after a few short years, we could not even say, "I love you."

Grief and anger welled up inside me. In desperation, I shared this with my father. He helped me see our relationship from Larry's point of view. I blamed my husband for not being sensitive to my needs, but was I sensitive to his? Had I been listening when he expressed his love in subtle, nonverbal ways? Had I become too proud and prickly to touch?

From that moment, I began to see Larry in a different light. I thought of the flush of first love that had inspired his poetic phrases. I began to see him with God's eyes, as the open, loving person he was meant to be.

God had brought us together for a purpose. I realized now that I had never surrendered myself to Larry completely, and that until I did that, God could never accomplish his purpose in our marriage.

As I said good-bye to my parents at the airport, tears streamed down my face. I hugged my father. "Pray for us," I whispered.

When I got back to England, I confronted Larry and told him honestly how I felt. It was the most painful moment in my life. The silence between us shattered into a thousand pieces as we poured out our hearts, revealing how deeply we had hurt one another. Through our tears, we made a commitment of total surrender—a vow we should have made years before. It was then that we truly became husband and wife.

Rebuilding our marriage was not an easy task. Tentatively we reached out, coming to know each other as if for the first time. We shared hurts and concerns and became vulnerable

to one another. We made small sacrifices, then big ones. Slowly, over time, God brought healing.

After five years in England, we decided to return to the United States and settle down. We talked about starting a family some day, but that day still seemed far away. Although our relationship was on the mend, we needed more time together.

We found a home in Minneapolis and a local church community that surrounded us with love. In their care, we grew spiritually, learning to look upward and outward rather than being preoccupied with ourselves. The sovereignty of God loomed larger in our lives; our priorities changed.

Rooted in love, our affection for one another grew. We enjoyed spending time together alone, sharing our dreams and deepest desires. Larry's dreams became mine, and mine his. I began free-lancing, which allowed me the freedom to write what interested me the most.

Finally we felt it was time for children. We had been married seven years, and although circumstances were not as ready as we would like them to be—Larry was uncertain in his job, my free-lancing meant less income—we knew the time was right.

Larry and I made the decision together, but as the moment drew near, I felt more alone. The seed would be planted inside me; I would carry our child and take on the primary responsibility for its care. Ultimately, I felt the decision was mine.

A deep-felt doubt surfaced in my mind: was it really God's will that we have a child? I had assumed that it was. Throughout the Bible, having children is described as a blessing and privilege, and the children themselves as God-given gifts. But I had not sought his leading specifically for this area of my life. This often happens as we face major decisions in

17

our lives; we seek his advice last, as if an afterthought—not for guidance, but for reassurance that what we've decided is OK with him.

If God was going to give me a child, I wanted to know why. Perhaps that sounds presumptuous. But we are told to seek and we will find answers. I had never sought so desperately for an answer to any other question.

I had recently visited friends at a lakefront cabin in northern Minnesota. That lake came to mind when I met the Lord in prayer. I imagined the serenity of the scene. It was a gorgeous golden afternoon. The autumn sun cast long shadows on the sandy shore.

In the middle of the lake, I saw a shining presence bidding me to come. As I drew near and stood opposite him face to face, I felt his love surround me. His eyes penetrated the depths of my being. The Lord knew why I had come. His words were clear and compelling, almost a command: "You are a child of God. I am your Father. You understand that relationship and all the love it involves. Now you should pass it on to your child."

I stood there staring for the longest time, wanting to know more. But that was all he said. It was up to me to unravel the meaning of those few words. His answer was meant to lead me on, to send me seeking in new directions.

What did I understand about my relationship with God? I knew that it had provided me with the opportunity to experience love in the fullest sense—joy beyond measure and profound pain. In Scripture, that unique relationship is described as parent-child; it must be so for a reason. Perhaps in the human relationship between parents and children we are meant to discover the same total experience.

It also occurred to me that by becoming a parent, I could learn more about the nature of God the Father. After all, that is our purpose here: to know God. Since God *is* love, we can learn to give and receive love more completely by knowing him better.

I did not question whether or not I should have children after that. I had my answer. There were other concerns now. Would I be able to withstand the pain of childbirth? Would Larry and I be able to adapt our life-style to care for a baby? "Trust me," said the Lord. "Trust me."

With my fears quieted, the idea of becoming parents no longer seemed threatening. It beckoned as an adventure. Since the time Larry and I had begun our life together, God had been working in our lives, opening our hearts, so that we could receive the full blessing of his special gift. The words on our wedding announcement came back to me: "The beginning of a new life is the wonder of creation."

2

A Time to Be Born

The miracle
and mystery of birth

"How do you feel?" I asked Larry. "Excited? Surprised?"

"Stunned." He was stretched out on the bed, staring at the ceiling. "I still can't believe it."

I couldn't either. When the nurse told me that my pregnancy test was positive, I nearly dropped the phone.

Only weeks before I had been wondering if I ever would get pregnant. After going off the Pill, I was told that it could take up to two years for my system to readjust so that I could become pregnant. Also I learned that older women are less fertile. Had I waited too long?

I discussed this with a friend who had been trying to have a baby for five years. She had tried everything—corrective surgery, fertility pills and drugs, taking her temperature to determine the time of ovulation.

One day she decided to throw away her pills and stop taking her temperature. "God spoke to me through Ecclesiastes," she said. "If there really is an appointed time for a child to be born, then I should let God choose the time."

My friend was right. If she could wait five years, I could wait five months. I relaxed after that and left the problem of pregnancy in God's hands.

There are many instances in the Bible of "timely" births. Luke tells us in his gospel about two babies who came unexpectedly to accomplish a particular purpose. Elizabeth and Zechariah were beyond childbearing age when an angel of the Lord revealed that God would send them a son. Zechariah was struck dumb because of his disbelief, but Elizabeth rejoiced. Their son became the prophet John the Baptist, who preached the coming of the Messiah.

Six months later the angel Gabriel visited Mary, a young virgin. When told that she would bear a son, she was amazed. "How can this happen?" Mary asked the angel. "I am not married." The angel assured her that the time had come for the Son of God to be born and it would happen even if it seemed impossible.

Mary hurried to share her secret with her cousin Elizabeth. When Elizabeth heard the good news, Luke says that the babe in her womb "leaped for joy" (Luke 1:44). Both prospective mothers knew that their sons were ordained by God to do great things.

Our children may not be born to change the course of history, but God has a purpose and plan for each child's coming. Unlike Mary and Elizabeth who knew immediately why their sons had been sent by God, we probably will wait years to know the God-given destiny of our children. We may never know.

As a new life stirs within her, every prospective mother daydreams about her child's future. "I suppose you want your child to be president of the United States," someone remarked to me. I smiled. It was a comment many pregnant

21

women hear; I might have made the same remark to an expectant friend.

But now that I was pregnant, I found I didn't think in those terms. I was more concerned with the kind of person my child would become rather than with what his or her mission in life would be. I hoped my baby would mature into a happy, caring individual, one who would embrace life openly and love others.

But daydreams formed a very small part of my thoughts. Most of the time I was preoccupied with being pregnant. At first it was difficult for me to comprehend that an actual human being was living inside me. I remember sitting in the obstetrics waiting room during the early months of pregnancy. The women around me were shaped like plump pears. I wasn't "showing" yet. I didn't look pregnant and I didn't feel pregnant until I was asked to lie down on an examination table while a nurse-midwife searched for the baby's heartbeat with a fetal monitor.

As she pressed the microphone to my abdomen, I was astonished by what I heard. "Th-rump. Th-rump." The tiny, pulsating sound seemed to fill the room. I couldn't stop laughing. "It's real! There's something in there!"

"Someone," corrected the nurse-midwife, glancing at her watch. "One hundred forty beats a minute. Heart rate is normal."

As the baby became more active in later months, it turned somersaults that sent ripples across my stomach. When my mind was far away, suddenly a throb from a kick or a punch from a little fist would startle me.

Once at a concert, I was absorbed in the romantic strains of a Rachmaninoff concerto. Suddenly my stomach turned over; I almost jumped out of my chair. Surely, I thought, someone must have noticed. But no one had. Everyone was gazing at the orchestra with stony stares, entranced with the performance.

At night when I lay in bed, relaxed, the baby was most active. "Ooooh, wow! Feel this," I would tell Larry as he was about to drift off to sleep. He stretched his hand on my tummy and smiled, then he rolled over. "You can't spend your whole life staring at your stomach," he said, yawning.

The physical sensation of pregnancy made the baby more real to me than to Larry. Like most husbands, he remained detached from the impending event.

"Melanie, Melantha, Melba, Melina." I thumbed through a baby book, searching for a name. "How do you like Melanie?"

"Huh?" Larry looked up briefly from a project that occupied him. "You're worried about names already?"

Then I came home with a secondhand crib. It was the only piece of furniture in the bare room that we'd designated as the nursery. Every time Larry passed that room, I noticed that he glanced at the crib out of the corner of his eye. The crib did more to convince him of the new baby than my pregnancy ever did. "I think we're committed," he said one day.

Three months before my due date, we began to take natural childbirth classes from Joy, a friend who was a nurse-midwife. I chose to deliver my baby without drugs because I wanted to be fully aware of the physical and emotional experience of giving birth. And I wanted Larry to share that miraculous moment with me rather than being relegated to the waiting room as my father had been. (When I was born in 1949, my father waited through the morning and night, pacing the floor of a busy New York hospital. Finally he grabbed the elbow of a passing doctor and asked about my mother. "Colmey? Colmey? Oh, yes," said the doctor. "I delivered that one hours ago. I think it was a girl.")

Fortunately times have changed. Husbands are encouraged to be active participants in the birth experience if they want to be—to support their wives and to witness one of the most dramatic events in both their lives.

As we went to natural childbirth classes, Larry learned to coach me through contractions. If I practiced my breathing exercises and conditioned my muscles, I was told that the pain during labor and delivery would be minimal. It would still hurt, but the preparation would make it easier and less painful. Could this really be possible?

I tried to be optimistic, but my expectations of childbirth were colored by harrowing descriptions in novels and movies. In Ernest Hemingway's short story "Indian Camp," a young husband is so horrified by the screams of his wife during labor that he slits his throat from ear to ear. These gloomy images and the fear of the unknown made the actual birth experience seem very frightening as my due date drew near.

As a Christian I had been taught that God ordained women to suffer pain during childbirth as a punishment for original sin, which offered me little comfort. I had come to know God as a loving Father who wanted the best for his children, not a vengeful judge who delighted in human suffering. This contrast bothered me.

It also disturbed Helen Wessel who decided to find out exactly what the Bible did say about childbirth. By comparing English translations of the Bible with the original Hebrew, she discovered that the "curse of Eve" tradition was based on a biased interpretation of Genesis 3:16-17 where the sin of Adam and Eve is recorded. In her book *The Joy of Natural Childbirth* (Harper & Row, 1976), Wessel quotes these verses from the King James Version:

Unto the woman he said, I will greatly multiply thy

sorrow (etsev) and thy conception; in *sorrow* (etsev) thou shalt bring forth children. . . . And unto Adam he said, . . . cursed is the ground for thy sake; in *sorrow* (etsev) shalt thou eat of it all the days of thy life.

Wessel points out that the Hebrew word *etsev*, which means "toil," is the same for the man and the woman. Adam and Eve were disciplined for breaking fellowship with God, but their punishment was designed to restore that fellowship. "Eve was to toil to bring forth the fruit of the body," writes Wessel. "Adam was to toil to bring forth the fruit of the ground, that they might learn to appreciate the good gifts that had been so freely given them before."

Giving birth is hard work; it is exhausting and it requires exertion. Certainly, complications can arise in abnormal births causing pain, but that is not what God intended. According to Wessel, there is not a single verse in the Bible that condemns women to suffer prolonged agony during childbirth as a punishment for sin.

She reminds us that women in primitive cultures have been delivering babies naturally for centuries with very little pain. Western culture, however, teaches that childbearing is tortuous and frightening. English translators simply carried over these cultural assumptions when they interpreted the Scriptures regarding childbirth.

Wessel maintains that childbirth is a natural event and if a woman is taught to give birth in harmony with the natural process, it can be an exhilarating experience—a blessing rather than a curse. Childbirth is not meant to be painful. On the contrary, Wessel believes it is one of God's most wonderful gifts.

When I thought of the discomfort that I would have to endure during childbirth, I clung to a promise that had carried me through many trials: "God is faithful, and he will not let you be tempted beyond your strength, but with the temptation will also provide the way of escape, that you may be able to endure it" (1 Cor. 10:13).

I was looking forward to receiving my child as a gift from God, but I had not thought of the process of giving birth as a God-given gift also. And yet it is. We are made in God's image. God is, above all else, the great Creator. Just as he first breathed life into a human being, so we are blessed with the creative ability to bring forth new life.

It is the unique, spiritual experience of creativity that gives childbirth dignity and beauty, says Wessel. Women who actively give birth without anesthesia feel an intense emotional "high" after normal birth. The reward for their hard work is all the sweeter because they have been fully aware of the total birth experience, from its fearful beginning to its euphoric climax.

By reading books like Helen Wessel's, I had prepared myself mentally for childbirth as much as I could. From my Lamaze training classes, I learned what would happen to my body during labor and delivery. Now there was nothing more to do but wait until the day arrived.

People say that a woman often can sense when her baby is about to be born. She has a premonition, a funny feeling. When my day arrived, having a baby couldn't have been further from my thoughts. My due date was still a month away. I was told to pack my suitcase—just in case. But I was busy, and there seemed to be plenty of time.

My sister Cindy and her husband, Allan, were visiting from New Zealand. I wanted them to meet our friends from church so I had invited 30 people that Sunday for a barbecue and volleyball game in our front yard.

I played volleyball vigorously, lunging over the sidelines

26

and jumping on tiptoe to spike the ball over the net. Everyone remarked on how physically fit I was at eight months pregnant. That pleased me because I had been determined to take my pregnancy in stride.

After our guests had strayed home, there was just enough time for a quick shower before we went to a concert at church that evening. Jon Byron, a Christian folksinger, was the featured performer. Byron's music filled the sanctuary as the congregation sang praises to the Lord:

We are the family of God,
Yes, we are the family of God.
And he's brought us together
To be one in him
That he might bring light to the world.

That refrain kept echoing in my mind as we left church and walked a few blocks to the Malt Shop. We laughed and joked as we walked, and I thought how good it was to be with Cindy and Allan and our good friends John and Susan.

At 10:30 the restaurant was still crowded with customers, but we managed to find a table for six. The waiter took our order: three malts and three milk shakes. We were debating the merits of malts versus milk shakes when suddenly I felt a strange sensation—a warm trickle of water on the chair beneath me. I tried to ignore it, but it came again. I turned to Cindy and whispered, "This must be impossible, but. . . ."

Her eyes grew wide. She looked at Susan, who grinned. My sister had two children of her own, and Susan was a pediatric nurse. They both recognized the first signs of labor.

Before I knew what was happening, they had whisked me off to the bathroom. I did not even have time to glance at Larry; I simply disappeared. The events that followed seemed to proceed with a momentum of their own.

Larry called our nurse-midwife friend, Joy, to see if she was at home. Minutes later we were sitting in her living room. "When did it happen? What does it feel like?" Joy asked. Her voice was methodical and detached as if this were just another lesson. She sat cross-legged on the couch as she always did when teaching us.

I remembered our Wednesday night lessons: Larry would pinch my earlobe to simulate the pain during a contraction, and I would respond with the appropriate breathing pattern. It was so abstract; I could have been learning algebra! Now it was no longer an intellectual exercise. After a quick examination, Joy confirmed that the baby was on the way.

Larry and I looked at each other in a state of shock. "We haven't finished our lessons. We haven't had our hospital tour. The nursery's not even ready." We both became delirious with laughter. "It can't be happening yet! We have a month to go!"

Joy told Larry to take me home and pack my things for the hospital. "Take your time," she said, trying to suppress a smile. When we got home, Cindy and Allan hurried around the house gathering up pajamas, socks, and magazines which they stuffed into my suitcase. I still hadn't felt a contraction, and I wondered why all these people were making such a fuss over me.

I called our parents to let them know we were going to the hospital. They appreciated the call but wondered why we were still at home. "I don't want to alarm you," said Larry's mom, "but if your waters have broken, you should get to the hospital as soon as possible."

As Larry sped down the freeway at midnight, I thought of a thousand things that needed doing. I threw up my hands in panic. "We haven't thought of a boy's name!" (I didn't intend to have a girl. What would I do with a daughter? I didn't like dolls or frilly dresses. It had to be a boy.)

When we arrived at the hospital, I felt a mild stab of pain like a menstrual cramp. Could that be a contraction? The pain went away as quickly as it came, and I forgot about it in the excitement.

We found our way to the maternity ward where a nurse undressed me and gave me a cotton gown to slip on. Then I was ushered into a small room and told to lie down. "Nothing should happen till tomorrow morning," said the nurse. She told Cindy and Larry to go home and that the hospital would call them if something developed.

I felt a rush of panic when I heard this because the crampy pains in my abdomen were coming more often now and I wanted Larry to be there in case I needed him. He assured me that he would go home to get the camera and be right back.

Then everyone left. The room was pitch-dark except for a strip of light that seeped under the door. "Try to sleep," the nurse had said when she closed the door. I did try to sleep, but the pain was becoming more intense.

Childbirth training had taught me to release the tension in my body by distracting by mind. Joy suggested that I bring a visual focal point—something that gave me a peaceful feeling, like a picture of a sunset. A friend of mine had used a picture of a lion for her focal point to boost her courage. This worked beautifully until she thought of the cowardly lion in *The Wizard of Oz*. Her resolve suddenly crumbled.

I had brought along a sunset picture, but it was buried in my suitcase. In the darkness I couldn't have seen it anyway.

I remembered the message of the sermon I had heard that morning: "Keep your eyes on Jesus." Of course, I thought, I could use Christ as my focal point.

In my imagination I pictured a sunlit forest, a tranquil scene where I often met the Lord in meditation. I walked along a path that was bordered by tall pines. There, in the middle of the path, stood Jesus. As I drew close to him, he took my hand.

We walked together as always, enjoying each other's company. For a moment I stepped back out of my body and became an objective observer, watching Christ and myself walking and talking. I often did this during meditation. But something was different this time. Instead of two figures strolling through the forest, I saw three. A small child walked beside me, holding my hand. It was a very vivid picture—the three of us walking happily together.

As I imagined this scene, Jon Byron's song came back to me:

We are the family of God,
Yes, we are the family of God.
And he's brought us together
To be one in him
That he might bring light to the world.

Jon Byron might have written those words especially for me.

All day I had felt a profound sense of being surrounded by God's family—playing volleyball with friends that afternoon, singing praises to God with his people, laughing at supper with my sister and brother-in-law. It was as if God had called together the community of believers for a special celebration to welcome a new little light into the world, a new member of his family.

As I was thinking about this, Cindy and Larry appeared at the door. I was glad to see them. The contractions were closer together; I knew it wouldn't be long.

I heard the nurse tell Larry that Joy was coming in. Larry and I had not dared to ask Joy to come to the hospital because we knew how busy she was. As a nurse-midwife student, she had a very hectic schedule of teaching and studies. She also had two children to care for. Sometimes when she was lecturing on childbirth, she would nod off to sleep in mid-sentence.

That night she was exhausted too. She told us later that she wanted to go to the hospital, but she was just too tired. As she drifted off to sleep, she prayed, "Lord, if you want me to be there, let me know in a very clear way." Just then, her pager went off. She called Fairview Hospital. Monica, the nurse-midwife on duty that night, asked if Joy wanted to assist at a delivery. The patient's name was Betsy Lee.

By the time Joy arrived, I was already in the transition stage of labor. I began to shiver uncontrollably. In minutes my body fluctuated from being chilled to overheated. Joy put a pillow between my legs which made lying on my side more comfortable. Her actions were efficient, confident, and reassuring. Again, I thought of how God was drawing together his family to surround me with his love.

While Joy left the room to consult with Monica, Larry started coaching me to work through the contractions. He asked me to tell him each time I felt the ebb and flow of a contraction. "Now . . . now," I whispered. The contractions were coming one after the other with almost no time in between.

Larry shook his head, bewildered. The average labor for

a first baby lasts 12 to 14 hours. After only two and a half hours, I was already having long, strong contractions, signaling the final stage of labor.

I was as confused as Larry. Everything was happening much faster than we had imagined. "I think I feel the urge to push."

Larry looked amazed. "Are you sure?"

"Yes. Yes." After I told him three times, he went to find Joy. She rushed in and examined my cervix, then she shouted for the nurse. I knew that the waiting was over. A few strong pushes and the baby would be out. Larry slipped on a green gown and surgical mask. Cindy squeezed my hand and wished me luck as my bed was wheeled into the delivery room.

Between contractions I was lifted from my bed onto the delivery table. My feet were slipped into stirrups and I was propped up at a 45-degree angle. Then I was told to push.

I took a deep breath, blew out quickly, and bore down with all my strength. Nothing happened. I rested until the next contraction came. I pushed harder. Still nothing happened.

Joy gave me a few last-minute lessons on pushing techniques. "Hold your breath as long as you can, then push."

I closed my eyes, concentrating on what she said. "Push!" came the command. "Harder! Harder!"

When I opened my eyes between pushes, I saw a circle of faces concentrating with me. Their foreheads were furrowed with effort, as if my struggle were theirs too. Together they shouted, "Push! Push!" Their consciousness seemed to melt into mine as we all focused on the single objective of pushing the baby through.

At that moment, the world didn't seem to exist beyond the walls of that delivery room, beyond the sound of those voices and the small pool of light overhead. As we all waited and watched, the baby began to emerge.

I heard someone say, "The heartbeat is low." An oxygen mask came down over my face. There was a sudden urgency in the voices around me, and I knew I had to push for all I was worth. So I bore down harder, holding my breath for what seemed like an eternity and straining as if I would burst. Suddenly the baby's head slid out in one quick motion. I expected to hear a howling cry or a piercing scream. Instead I heard a soft whimper.

"It's a girl," Joy announced. "She has lots of hair."

The baby was wrapped in a blanket to keep warm, then she was placed across my stomach so that we stared at each other face to face. I had been told that a newborn's head often is misshapen after it has been squeezed through the birth canal. The features are sometimes squashed and dis-figured. "You will be shocked," people said, "when you see how ugly your baby is."

I was amazed, but not by her ugliness. As I gazed into the wide, quiet eyes that looked up at me, I was breathless with the beauty of this little being. Her features were deli-cately shaped: she had a heart-shaped face and tiny rosebud lips. She was perfect in every way.

We named her Brenna, which means "raven-haired" in Gaelic. She had fine, dark hair like her father. I looked up at Larry. Above the surgical mask there were tears in his eyes. Neither one of us could speak.

The nurse said, "You can touch her." My uncertainty must have showed as I reached out tentative fingertips. I was filled with a sense of awe. For eight months I had waited for this meeting, and now I felt paralyzed. Did I dare touch her? In my mind this tiny creature was merely a dream, intangible, elusive, without form or substance. As she grew inside my body, a deep, silent intimacy developed between us, but still I could not picture her as a person.

Now as she lay on my stomach staring at me, she searched my face with curiosity and wonder. Her eyes seemed to say, "So this is my mother." Her world had been dreamlike too: cradled in the shifting sea of the womb, rocked by the rhythm of my breathing. She looked as astonished to see me for the first time as I was to see her.

There would be time for touching and time to get acquainted later but not now. We had only a few seconds together before the nurse took Brenna away. Because she was premature, she had to be put under oxygen immediately.

The atmosphere in the delivery room changed now from tension and concentration to celebration. I felt ethereal and light-headed. Everyone was grinning. Joy hugged me. My sister was waiting for me in the corridor. She was jubilant. I knew that she was happy for me, but she seemed to be bursting with a special joy of her own.

Later she told me that her deepest desire was to be with me when my baby was born. It was a way, she said, of God's restoring all the moments of sharing with me and the family that she had missed over the past seven years while living abroad.

I marveled at how perfect God's will had been in choosing the time for Brenna to be born. If she had arrived a month later, as predicted, Cindy and Allan would have been halfway around the world in New Zealand. Joy wouldn't have been there to deliver the baby because she had plans to be on vacation then.

Just as God had chosen the perfect day for Brenna's birth, I also began to realize that she had come at the right time in my life. Years earlier I had been too full of professional ambition to make room for a child. I did not have the depth

34

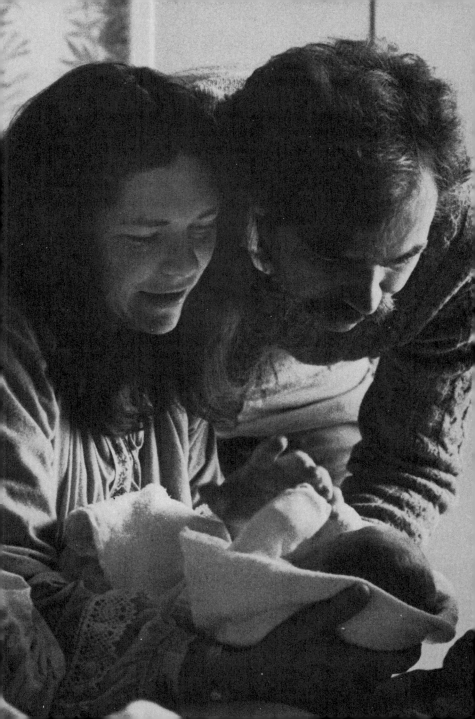

of experience or capacity for love I needed to surrender my self-interest and become a mother.

In the next few days, as Brenna nestled in my arms, I discovered that I was ready to embrace and nurture a new human being in a way I hadn't been before. Every time I gazed into those wistful eyes, tears welled up from some hidden depth within me.

"I have a daughter." I kept whispering that phrase over and over in my mind like a litany, savoring the sound and the mystery of its meaning.

3

A Time to Embrace

Home from the hospital

As we drove home from the hospital on that sunny day in July, the sky seemed especially blue, the trees shone with a brilliance I never noticed before. I felt giddy, full of exuberance and joy. I wanted to wrap my arms around the world and hold it close.

"It's like falling in love."

Larry looked at me askance.

I tried to explain how magical the last 24 hours had been. During my five days in the maternity ward, I had been separated from Brenna. She was kept in a nursery at the end of the corridor. On the sixth day I was allowed to share the same room with her on the pediatric ward as she recuperated from jaundice.

We were left completely alone. I spent hours taking long, leisurely looks at her, absorbed by her every movement, transfixed by her steady gaze. Already an invisible bond began to pull our separate beings into a mysterious sense of oneness.

Larry couldn't understand this. Our newborn baby couldn't

talk or express herself. How could she possibly communicate? How could you actually have a relationship with her?

When Larry and I had discussed parenthood, he said he would *really* begin to take an interest in the baby when she was about nine months old. By that time she would have developed a personality and she would be able to do things. Things meant crawling, laughing, and saying "dada." Until then he thought the baby wouldn't be much fun. How could he relate to her if she couldn't respond to him?

Most new fathers think along these lines. The newborn infant is cute and curious, but still an object, a helpless entity to be diapered, burped, and fed. Research reveals that, contrary to the myth of maternal instinct, many mothers share these same feelings of detachment and strangeness toward their babies.

As I sat propped up in my hospital bed watching TV courses on infant care during those first few days, my main concerns were how to bathe the baby, how to fold a diaper, and how to master the art of breast-feeding. I was told to hold the baby like a football, tucking her under my right arm as she sucked on my right breast. If the "football hold" didn't work, the nurses suggested a dozen different ways to get the job done.

But there weren't any courses on how to form a relationship with your baby. When Joy came in to check my episiotomy the day after delivery, she brought me a box of diaper pins, plastic pants, nipples, disposable bottles, and a baby album. I surveyed the paraphernalia strewn over the bed and shrugged my shoulders. "But Joy," I said, searching and uncertain, "I really don't feel like a mother."

She smiled. "Don't worry. It's not love at first sight for most mothers. The relationship evolves, like any other relationship. You have to get to know one another."

38

When Brenna and I spent time together on that last day, without nurses' advice or TV lectures, I did begin to feel a quiet blossoming of intimacy between us. I could not fully explain the elusive quality of bonding to Larry because I did not understand it myself.

I said simply, "You will see what I mean when you spend some time with her."

Larry had only enjoyed brief glimpses of his daughter. While I was in the hospital, he was busy finishing Brenna's nursery. Because she had come a month early, we were totally unprepared. Friends from church had brought bags of clothes, toys, and all the nursery items that we needed for our homecoming.

During our first two hours home, the baby slept quietly in her bassinet. "Well," said Larry, strutting across the bedroom looking proud and pleased, "fatherhood isn't so bad."

When Brenna woke up, we had our first crisis. During my six days in the hospital, I had never actually changed a diaper. The nurses had always courteously whisked the baby away to change her. Now, faced with my first opportunity for hands-on experience, I nearly panicked.

Larry held up Dr. Spock's baby care manual, and we both scrutinized the diagram. Brenna only weighed five and a half pounds. She was so small that a newborn diaper had to be folded over and over again to fit her. We argued about which way to fold the diaper and how to stick in the pins.

Brenna looked up at us quizzically. "She's wondering how she ended up at this house," said Larry. "These people don't know what they're doing!" We both looked at each other and laughed. Here we were, college graduates, reasonably intelligent people, feeling like complete fools as parents.

We were laughing, but subconsciously I really did doubt my capability to care for a baby. People had always said,

"Larry will be such a wonderful father." No one had ever said I would make a good mother. The first weeks at home were hectic. Day and night drifted into a dreamlike existence as I slept fitfully, waiting to feed the baby at a moment's notice. I had several frightening nightmares during this time.

Once I dreamt that I put a naked baby in a pot of boiling water to make soup. The baby decomposed before my eyes. Suddenly I realized what I had done. Desperately I tried to put the baby together again. I felt a tremendous sense of guilt, and I hoped that Larry would not discover what I'd done.

I looked as pale as a sheet the next day when our neighbor told me his grandmother had been kept in an oven when she was born prematurely in rural Kentucky. It was a common practice to incubate the baby that way until he reached full term. I could easily imagine putting Brenna in the oven and later turning the knob for supper, forgetting that she was there.

When I shared my anxieties about baby care with my pediatrician, she echoed Dr. Spock's advice: trust yourself. Babies are tough; you can't do much to hurt them. It is not uncommon for mothers to harbor feelings of inadequacy and even resentment toward a newborn. Just as pregnancy is fraught with ambivalent emotions, so motherhood may seem awesome and threatening. I was told to relax and enjoy Brenna.

Still, it was not easy to think of her as tough. She was so tiny that she could easily fill a shoe box with room to spare. "She looks like a little bird that has fallen out of the nest," Larry said, swallowing her in his arms. The skin hung in folds on her thin bones. Her ears were pressed flat against her head like leaves because the cartilage had not developed yet. Larry shook his head. "She would never survive in the wild."

I learned later that an infant's physical characteristics are designed to insure his survival—even in the wild. The small size of a newborn, the chubby cheeks, button nose, and uncoordinated body movements give infants a vulnerable and helpless look that elicits a protective response from an adult caregiver. The Danish ethologist Konrad Lorenz found that this was true for animal babies as well as human infants.

Researchers have also discovered that infants are equipped with an inborn ability to teach their mothers how to mother. A baby begs to be held; his tiny body naturally molds into his mother's lap. Set free from the closed environment of the womb, he longs to be caressed, he snuggles and clings, trying to merge with her again.

Through an elaborate system of tactile movements and facial gestures, the baby engages the mother in a dialogue of silent communication. Margaret Mahler, the child psychologist, describes this choreographed conversation as "mutual cueing"—"a circular process of interaction established very early between mother and infant by which they 'empathetically' read each other's signs and signals and react to each other."

The social smile is a clear example of this. An infant smiles with pleasure when he recognizes his mother's face; Mom smiles back. Even a blind baby who has never seen a smile will automatically search for his mother's eyes and smile when he hears her voice.

Eye-to-eye contact is an important part of mother-infant communication. For newborns, most of their visual landscape is fuzzy and out of focus. They can only see objects clearly about eight inches away, the average distance between a baby and his mother's face while feeding at breast or bottle. Gradually the newborn's field of vision broadens to the edge of his mother's face and beyond.

But at first the newborn's whole visual world is encompassed by his mother's face. He scrutinizes every detail, studying the nose and mouth and eyes. By two or three months the infant fixes his attention on his mother's eyes as she talks to him. Because his gaze is so intense, the mother too begins to lose herself in her infant's eyes. Mother and infant become so totally absorbed in one another that they create what Mahler calls a "symbiotic membrane," a protective shield that surrounds them both, drawing them into mutual dependence.

Lovers do this when they lock eyes and melt into each other. As they merge into one, even their thoughts become identical. "How did you know what I was thinking?" one whispers to the other. The empathy of lovers is a rare thing; most of our relationships are casual and impersonal. We are embarrassed to gaze directly into each other's eyes and risk intimacy.

Looking back at those early days of motherhood, I can barely remember the sleepless nights, frustrations, and fear of failure. What I remember most are the precious, timeless moments when I held Brenna to my breast and gazed into her eyes. She would look at me so directly that I could see my whole face reflected in the tiny pupil of her eye, no bigger than a teardrop.

Months later when I went shopping, I would place Brenna on a bench in her carrier seat. I went about my business, confident that no matter how far I wandered, Brenna would not lose sight of me. "Your daughter hasn't taken her eyes off you," strangers remarked. Once someone said, "I can't help but notice how your daughter adores you." I glanced down at Brenna; her eyes were fixed on me.

Babies need affection and focused attention for emotional nourishment as much as they need food to grow. But I did not realize how much I would enjoy basking in my baby's love. To be adored, to be the most important person in her world, was gratifying and very special.

Brenna adored her father too. She became just as fascinated by Larry's face as mine. This was a measure of the closeness Larry had cultivated with his daughter. Breast-feeding books always include advice to fathers: don't feel shut out from the "nursing couple"; there are other ways you can care for your baby.

At night Larry picked up Brenna from the crib and brought her into our bed for feeding. He changed her and held her in his arms when she was fussy. Often she would drift off to sleep while lying on his stomach. When she had indigestion, the warmth of bodily contact calmed her. She would lie like a limp rag doll, arms and legs hanging over the side of his broad chest. Together they were a picture of contentment.

My husband quickly forgot his protest that babies couldn't communicate. Had he ever doubted that this tiny human being was capable of love? Now a new complaint arose: "When she gets bigger, she won't be able to lie on my stomach. Some day she won't even be huggable!"

I thought about this when we went with a friend to Thanksgiving dinner. It was a small family reunion of parents and adult children. As my friend's father said good-bye to her, I could see the longing in his eyes, the tenderness and tug of his heart as she kissed him quickly and danced out the door, beyond his grasp. She was no longer his little girl.

That same drama must have been acted out many times before by my own father and me, yet I had never recognized it. I thought of the times my father came up behind me and hugged me while I was doing the dishes on a visit home. Or he would suddenly kiss me and look straight into my eyes. "It's so nice to have you home," he would whisper.

I wondered why he couldn't say, "I love you," because that is what he meant. And I wondered why I grew tense and standoffish in his embrace. Why wouldn't I let him demonstrate his love for me, and why couldn't I openly express my love for him? Larry was right. I wasn't huggable anymore.

This realization made me marvel even more at the vulnerability and complete trust of babies. You can hug them as tight as you want; you can kiss and cuddle them. They thrive on the least bit of attention. Their appetite for love seems insatiable.

Perhaps that is why Jesus said we must be like little children to enter the kingdom of God. Infants aren't aware of themselves as individuals yet; they haven't built barriers that separate them from other human beings. Even at three and four years old, children are completely open with their love. They'll start conversations with strangers or hug someone they've never seen before.

God's deepest desire is to have a personal relationship with us, to hold us in his arms like a loving parent. In order to know God as our heavenly Father, we have to rediscover our childlike nature of openness and trust. We need to be huggable.

Paul tells us in Romans 8:15 that we should call God *Abba,* the Greek word for father or dad. As God's children, we are also instructed to think of the maternal qualities of our divine parent. In Isaiah God promises his chosen people, "You shall suck, you shall be carried upon her hip, and dandled upon her knees. As one whom his mother comforts, so I will comfort you" (Isa. 66:12-13).

A new Christian often experiences feelings of euphoria when he first discovers that God's love is personal and real, meant just for him. As a spiritual newborn, he looks up into his Creator's face with adoration. He recognizes that God is the source of perfect love. He is fully aware that he is a child resting in his Father's embrace, relying on his Father's strength.

One day he grows to be independent. He forgets the Father who made him; he is no longer trusting. When he ceases to seek God's face and humble himself as a child, he loses that closeness, his resting place. He wanders away, he falls, he hurts himself, he hurts the Father.

This constant conflict between dependence and independence haunts us all our lives. It characterizes our psychological journey from infanthood to the discovery of self, and it is the central focus of our spiritual experience. Psychologist Louise J. Kaplan calls this tension the "dilemma between oneness and separateness." "Whenever the challenge of separateness becomes too great," she writes, "we all long to bring back the primary bliss of oneness. This basic human longing to refind our core wholeness is the essence of religion and poetry and the essence of the ecstasies of perfect love."

In *Oneness and Separateness* (Simon & Schuster, 1978), Kaplan refers to our first experience of wholeness as a "heavenly dialogue of merging, body-molding unity." It is a oneness based on unconditional love, freely given and freely received. That is exactly the kind of love that God offers us. He asks us to come to him with open arms ready to receive the goodness he wants to give.

Why have we lost this vision of God as Father? Why don't we experience the immediacy of his presence in our prayers? So often our communication is one-way. We do all the talking; he listens. What of the heavenly dialogue?

It is possible to still the stirrings of the soul, to grow so quiet that you can hear the very heartbeat of God. "Draw near to God," says James, "and he will draw near to you" (James 4:8).

It occurred to me that I had never told God that I loved him. I had sung his praises, given him offerings, and worshiped him, but I had never said, "I love you." In my imagination, I pictured God as a parent. I crawled into his lap and whispered these words in his ear. And then I let his love flow freely around me. I felt a deep, deep closeness with the Lord, a melting away of barriers, an experience of wholeness and well-being.

I hugged Brenna more often after that. And I decided the next time I saw my father, I would not wait for him to hug me; I would throw my arms around him first.

46

4

A Time to Secure

Building a bond of love

Psychologists say that parents create a "holding environment" for their baby by undergirding him with constant care and support. By the loving inflections in their voices, by the tenderness of their touch, by their reassuring looks, they sustain an infant beyond the physical presence of their embrace. This was the next step in our relationship: securing the bond between us.

For the first few weeks, Brenna slept in a bassinet in our bedroom. To my sensitive ears, the sound of her faint breathing seemed magnified; the slightest sniffle or cough startled me. When she suddenly went quiet, my heart stopped. Had she choked or smothered? My cousin's baby had died of crib death, with no explanation or warning, and that worried me.

"Don't mother yourself to death," Larry teased. I knew I was being overanxious, but I couldn't help myself. Even though we were physically separated, the emotional attachment between me and my baby was so strong that she still seemed like an extension of my own body. When she cried,

I felt the sudden surge of milk moving in my breasts; even a change of her breathing pattern could cause my uterus to contract with concern.

I discussed this with experienced mothers. They laughed, remembering their own early weeks of worry. The solution was simple. The only way I was going to get any sleep was to move the baby into another room—far enough not to be wakened by her breathing, but close enough to hear her cry when she really did need me.

The first night that Brenna slept alone was traumatic for us both. I couldn't get used to the absolute silence in our bedroom. I was accustomed to hearing some sound, some evidence of Brenna's being there. Now that she was gone, I felt a gnawing emptiness inside. "Is this what it will feel like when she goes away to camp?" I wondered out loud.

Larry laughed. "She's only 15 feet away!"

Brenna was lonely too. We thought she would be pleased to have a room of her own, but to her the nursery seemed like a sea of empty space. She missed the constant sound of our conversation and the low hum of the radio. The close, comforting walls of the bassinet had given way to cold emptiness. We found her the next morning huddled in a ball in the middle of the crib, looking lost and abandoned.

The next night we put Brenna to sleep in the corner of her crib, hemmed in by the bumper pad on one side and by a wall of stuffed animals on the other. She felt more secure in the confined space. Gradually, as she grew older, she stretched out her fingers and explored the menagerie of stuffed animals and dolls that ringed her crib.

A red gingerbread man was propped in the corner. Next to him stood a crocheted rabbit, a woolly lamb, a yellow bunny, a doll dressed in gingham, and Sloobie, a bean bag character with a blue tuft of hair and red felt feet. One by

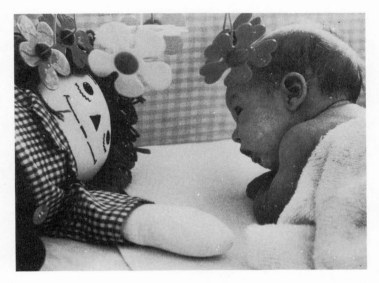

one, the stuffed playmates became her friends. She cooed to
them and caressed them and later told them stories. They
kept her company until Larry and I returned in the morning.

"Let me go in first," Larry would beg. We both relished
walking into Brenna's nursery in the morning. When she
saw us, she popped up from the covers and grinned, her eyes
sparkling. Brenna's first smile of the day was always her
brightest. "It's great to see you," she seemed to say. "I've
missed you through the night."

Brenna's well-being depended on her certain faith that
we would be there because we had greeted her every morning
of her young life. By building up trust day by day, we let her
know that she could count on us not to abandon her. Secure
in this knowledge, she felt surrounded by love even when we
weren't there to hold her.

Giving Brenna a sense of inner security became all important as she developed an awareness of herself as an individual,

a person in her own right who existed apart from us. Without this security, she would not have been free to discover the world on her own.

When we put Brenna in the bathtub, she was surprised and terrified. Her eyes grew wide and her mouth dropped open in an elongated "O" as she felt the strange sensation of water lapping at her skin. We tried to ease her in gently: I handed her to Larry, and he lowered her slowly into his lap. But she was still overwhelmed with fright.

Little by little she lost her fear of taking a bath in the big tub and learned to enjoy it. With Larry supporting her, she would float on her back, legs and arms outstretched, her clenched fists finally relaxed. Larry flipped her over on her stomach, and she started to kick. After her first tentative "thunk," she began to kick with both legs, amazed by the effect she had on the water.

After she discovered the pleasure of splashing, she was soon venturing out of Larry's arms to explore other aspects of her new environment. She put her hand flat against the side of the tub and let it slide on the slippery porcelain; she poked her fingers up the faucet and chased her sputtering dolphin in circles. Occasionally she reached too far and suddenly lost her balance, gasping with surprise as Larry caught her. She clung to him, struggling to regain her composure before she launched out on her own again.

This was the pattern of all Brenna's learning experiences. As long as we were there for support, she felt confident and daring. If she succeeded, we praised her; if she failed, we put the shattered pieces of her self-esteem back together. We restored her wholeness by providing a resting place where she could feel safe and secure, impervious to danger, protected, at peace.

As an infant pulls away from his mother to establish his

own identity, he still looks to her for rootedness. Louise Kaplan describes the process in this way: "The mother's presence is like a fixed light that gives the child the security to move out safely to explore the world and then return safely to harbor." The normal child builds up an experience of "inner mother" that orients him in the world and allows him to become independent.

"For a human baby," writes Kaplan, "there is no environment without a mother." The same thing can be said about our relationship with God: for a Christian there is no environment without Christ. No matter how far a Christian wanders, Christ remains fixed and permanent, offering a refuge. The Holy Spirit is the Christian's inner mother, always orienting him toward God.

"The eternal God is your dwelling place," Moses told the Israelites as they wandered in the desert, "and underneath are the everlasting arms" (Deut. 33:27). As the model parent, God provides a holding environment for his children by his constant care and support. We are encouraged to provide the same security for our own children.

In the Old Testament God's steadfast love for Israel is compared to a shepherd's care for his sheep. The most explicit description of this relationship is found in the 23rd Psalm. David, a shepherd himself, appreciates the diligence and benevolent care that God demonstrates in watching over his children. As parents, there is much that we can learn about the qualities of a good caregiver in this poem:

The Lord is my shepherd,
    I shall not want;
he makes me lie down in green pastures.
He leads me beside still waters;
    he restores my soul.

He leads me in paths of righteousness
for his name's sake.
Even though I walk through the
valley of the shadow of death,
I fear no evil;
for thou art with me;
thy rod and thy staff,
they comfort me.
Thou preparest a table before me
in the presence of my enemies;
thou anointest my head with oil,
my cup overflows.
Surely goodness and mercy shall follow me
all the days of my life;
and I shall dwell in the house of the Lord
forever.

In his book *A Shepherd Looks at Psalm 23* (Zondervan, 1970), Phillip Keller explains how every detail in David's psalm points to God's perfect provision for his loved ones. First, the intimacy of the relationship is established. *The Lord is my shepherd.* God is our master, our manager, our owner; as such he is willing to sacrifice everything for our welfare. He calls us by name and attends to our every need. His greatest happiness is seeing us thrive and flourish.

I shall not want. A conscientious shepherd spares no pains to supply his sheep with the best of everything: fine grazing, clean water, shelter from storms, protection from predators. He will risk his life and, if necessary, lay down his life in defense of his flock.

He makes me lie down in green pastures. In a good shepherd's care the sheep rest content, knowing their protector is nearby. Sheep are so timid, says Keller, that they refuse to lie down unless they are free from fear and hunger. Certainly this is true of children: they can only relax when all their basic needs have been met.

Just as a shepherd watches his flock, a loving mother always has an ear open to hear the cries of her infant. Even when she's sleeping, she'll jump up at a moment's notice. As a child learns that his mother is always there to answer his needs, he learns to trust himself more and more to her care.

He restores my soul. Security involves more than meeting basic needs. There are also times of distress that require special care. Even in the Good Shepherd's care, children of God are overwhelmed sometimes by life's disappointments and defeats. With David, we've all cried out, "Why are you cast down, O my soul?" (Ps. 42:11). Keller explains that *cast down* is a shepherd's term for a sheep that is turned over on its back and can't get up. When a sheep is rendered helpless like this, it is easy prey for vultures and wolves. The shepherd must come quickly to the sheep's rescue and set it on its feet again.

Like sheep, children often find themselves in helpless predicaments. An alert parent comes quickly and eagerly to the aid of the little one, restoring his confidence and fragile sense of self. This requires patience and sensitivity. Toddlers ask for help incessantly; mother must kiss their "owies" even if they don't hurt. Teenagers, on the other hand, shun help, and a parent must be acutely aware of his child's needs to sense when something is wrong.

I fear no evil; for thou art with me. David's picture of the faithful shepherd suggests that God not only hears our cries of distress, but he also goes ahead to make our way as smooth as possible, anticipating dangers that we cannot foresee. Every year shepherds guide their sheep through dark valleys to the sunlit meadows of the mountaintops for summer grazing.

From experience the shepherd knows the safest, gentlest route. He has already gone ahead to prepare the tableland, rooting out the poisonous weeds and scouting for signs of predators.

Parents also use their wisdom and experience to protect a child from unnecessary risks. Just as they "baby-proof" the house, putting poisons out of reach to keep a one-year-old from hurting himself, so they continue to go ahead of their child, trying to make his life easier by teaching him how to cope with difficult situations before he confronts them. Of course, it is impossible to avoid all problems, but some can be avoided by careful planning.

Thy rod and thy staff, they comfort me. The shepherd uses two tools to guide his flock: the rod and the staff. According to Keller, a shepherd's rod symbolizes his strength and authority. It is used as a weapon to ward off danger and as an instrument of discipline. "He who spares the rod hates his son," said Solomon, "but he who loves him is diligent to discipline him" (Prov. 13:24).

The staff symbolizes the shepherd's compassion. Gently he uses his staff to keep the sheep in line, drawing them close to the flock and guiding them on the proper path. A child feels a deep sense of comfort when he knows that someone who has his best interests at heart is gently but firmly reminding him: "This is the way, walk in it" (Isa. 30:21).

David had experienced such wonderful care as a child of God that he ends his poem on a triumphant note of praise: *My cup overflows! Surely goodness and mercy shall follow me all the days of my life!* This is exactly what Christ intended when he said that he came that we might have life and have it more abundantly. Secure in the hands of a loving Lord, a Christian can enjoy life to the fullest, free of anxiety and fear.

Christ called himself the Good Shepherd and the Lamb of God. In this amazing paradox lies the mystery of God's great love for us. In order to identify with humanity and experience the struggles that we all face, God through Christ took on human form; the shepherd became a lamb. Christ suffered like us, he was tempted, he was tried, and for one terrible moment he was forsaken. Because of this, he understands us completely and is able to care for us with tenderness and compassion.

Because of this, he can truly say, "I know my own and my own know me, as the Father knows me and I know the Father" (John 10:14-15). A caregiver must have intimate knowledge of his charge in order to provide the best care, which is why God's love is perfect. Only God knows every human being's secret heart. "Your Father knows what you need before you ask him," said Jesus (Matt. 6:8).

I thought about this one day as I stood at Brenna's bedroom door watching her rouse for her afternoon feeding. I knew from experience that she would rub the sleep from her eyes and cry from hunger. I was so certain of this that I could anticipate it and be there even before she felt a need to cry. How much more completely must the Lord know us! And how much more attentive he is!

No matter how conscientious we are as parents, we are bound to fall down on the job. Our babies' cries are heard in the midst of conflicting demands and busy schedules. Sometimes we become frantic trying to comfort our children when we need comfort ourselves. That is when a Christian parent needs to turn to God to restore his own equilibrium.

This was brought home to me when Brenna was about six months old. She was going through an anxiety stage. As babies become more independent, they are often frightened and cling to their mothers before finally letting go. Brenna wouldn't let me out of her sight; she was desperate if I left the room. Soon she would be able to crawl away from me, and she needed to be reassured that I would always be there, still the fixed, permanent center of her ever-expanding world.

It was a difficult time for me too. As Brenna became more active and independent, no longer needing my quiet embraces, I also felt a growing independence from her. I became impatient with her demands. Why does she need me so much? I wondered. Why can't her father stop her crying? Why must it always be me?

One day during that period, I found myself distraught, desperate, needing comfort. I went to the Lord in meditation. I imagined meeting him in my familiar sunlit forest.

Usually I could see him waiting for me on the path bordered by tall pines. This time for some reason I could not find him. For a moment I felt a stab of panic. Where was he? Didn't he know how much I needed him?

Then, through my tears, I saw him waiting as always with outstretched arms. I buried my face on his shoulder, crying. He stroked my hair softly and wiped my tears. I felt ashamed. Why had I been so demanding and impatient, so childish?

Childish. I suddenly realized how Brenna felt when she was tired and overwrought, falling to pieces at the end of the day. "As a father pities his children," said David, "so the Lord pities those who fear him. For he knows our frame; he remembers that we are dust" (Ps. 103:13-14). If God could accept my weakness, why couldn't I accept by baby daughter's? Why couldn't I recognize her frailty and be glad that she came to me for comfort?

There was another question that disturbed me even more. Why couldn't I accept my own weakness? Adults place such importance on self-sufficiency and being self-contained that they are afraid to admit their inadequacies and reach out to others for support.

That night I tiptoed into Brenna's room. Before dropping off to sleep, she held her head up, eyeing her stuffed animals and dolls. She reached for Sloobie, fingering his blue tufts of hair. She gave him a love bite and tucked him under her chest. Then she reached for her woolly lamb and pulled him under too. Next she grabbed her rabbit and gingerbread man, and finally her ginghamed doll. On this mound of stuffed playmates, she fell asleep, sucking her thumb.

"How uncomfortable!" I thought. But Brenna couldn't have been happier. Hugging her friends close, she slept well, comforted and content. It reminded me of a Charlie Brown cartoon: "Security is knowing you're not alone."

5

A Time to Give

Loving, teaching, disciplining, and forgiving

"What man of you, if his son asks him for bread, will give him a stone?" said Jesus. "Or if he asks for a fish, will give him a serpent?" (Matt. 7:9-10). We all want the best for our children. We give them good things daily and shower them with gifts to make them happy. But are our gifts appropriate? Do we always know what our children need?

Brenna's first Christmas was spent with her cousins, Christopher, three, and Timmy, one. Surrounded by admiring relatives, the boys ripped through boxes and bows, discovering and discarding one expensive toy after another. At last they found something that held their attention. On a whim, my father decided to give them two old stocking hats that had been buried in the closet for years.

Christopher pulled the cap over his eyes and ran wildly in circles, crashing into furniture and rolling on the floor. Timmy played peek-a-boo with his. "You never know what kids will like," we all shook our heads, completely baffled. At our feet Brenna amused herself by crinkling wrapping paper and draping ribbon around her neck.

It is not easy for an adult to look at the world through an infant's eyes or to dance dizzily with a toddler, ecstatic with simple joys. And yet that is exactly what we must do.

Getting behind the eyes of a child is the fundamental skill of good parenthood, according to Dr. James Dobson, a Christian psychologist. "It is this awareness of his world," says Dobson in his book *Hide or Seek* (Revell, 1974), "that permits a parent (or teacher or grandparent) to hold the child when he is threatened, or love him when he is lonely, or teach him when he is inquisitive, or discipline him when he knows he is wrong."

In order to love, teach, and discipline, which require giving every day, it is even more essential to know our children's needs than it is when giving them gifts on special occasions. We can guess wrong once or twice at Christmas; our children will weather the disappointment. But our daily pattern of loving, teaching, and disciplining shapes their lives and determines what kind of people they will be. To these three, I will add one more: forgiveness. Nothing is more important than these gifts and the way we give them.

The gift of love

Love can be extremely easy to give, or terribly difficult. My mother grew up in a family of girls. Her first two children were daughters, and she was comfortable raising us. The third child was a boy, my brother, John. John confounded my mother from the day he was born. There was always a distance between John and Mom. She wasn't quite sure how to express her affection or tame his wild spirit.

Because he was a boy, she was more protective of him,

worrying about what trouble he would get into and warning him constantly about dangers to avoid. One day my brother refused to wear his coat to school even though my mother warned that he would catch cold.

"You're always telling me that," John whined.

She explained that her instructions were for his benefit. As his mother, she had to protect him and keep him healthy. "What do you think a mother is for?"

"A mother is to love me," said John.

I'm sure my mother was stunned by this. She was prudent enough not to be defensive and shout back: "Of course I love you. That's why I asked you to wear your coat!" Instead she wondered why John didn't perceive her protective attitude as a sign of affection. She thought about changing the way she communicated love to him.

She talked to her sister, who had raised a son. "Boys aren't any different than girls," said my aunt. "They need to be touched and caressed and kissed good-night." This was a revelation to my mother who thought her son's masculinity would be compromised if she cuddled him. As soon as she started to demonstrate her love in direct, visible ways, John responded to my mother with greater warmth, and he began to respect her authority because he knew that her requests emanated from a heart of love.

In all relationships, whether between friends, husband and wife, or parents and children, love must be expressed in words and actions in order to grow. Otherwise, indifference sets in. A husband dashes out the door and forgets to kiss his wife good-bye; it becomes a habit. He comes home late every night, never allowing enough time to play with the baby. Soon they are strangers spinning silently in separate orbits.

How God must be grieved by the offhanded way we treat each other! He made us in his image: to express tenderness and to develop deep, intimate relationships. I once saw a four-year-old beg for her mother's attention while the mother babbled on mindlessly in conversation. "Mom! Mom!" the little girl shouted. Exasperated, she finally clamped her hands around her mother's face and stared at her eyeball to eyeball. "Oh, did you want something?" the mother asked, as if in a daze.

Just as bad habits can let love die, good habits fuel the warmth of a relationship. Spending time with one another, demonstrating love through physical contact, and giving each other focused attention are all ways to deepen intimacy.

"The only gift is a portion of thyself," said Ralph Waldo Emerson, "thou must bleed for me." Love means putting the other person first, which often takes sacrifice. On a fine day in September, Larry and I were driving along the southern shore of Lake Superior. We had a long drive ahead of us, and I did not show much enthusiasm when Larry decided to pull off the road and take a stroll along the beach. "We won't be long," he promised, as he slung the baby onto his back.

"It's windy. Be sure to put her hood up to protect her ears," I said, falling into the worrying routine that had always annoyed me in my mother. Larry trekked a half mile down the beach before I caught up with him. He slipped Brenna out of the carrier and plopped her on the sand.

"You're not going to let her play in the sand!" He completely ignored my protest that sand in Brenna's overalls would make a mess in the car. Off came her jacket and socks. Brenna burrowed her toes in the beach. She grabbed a fistful of sand and threw it up in the air, letting it shower over her face.

Then I watched in horror as Larry slipped off his shoes and socks and rolled up his trousers. "You're not going to take her in the water! She'll catch cold!" Colds for mothers mean sleepless nights, constant worry and bother. I was more concerned with the inconvenience it would cause me than I was with Brenna's health.

Larry wasn't concerned with either. He simply wanted to make his daughter happy. "Look," Larry said, dangling her bare feet in the water. "She loves it!" Brenna giggled as the waves tickled her feet; she pumped her arms up and down with excitement.

"Thou must bleed for me. . . ." Cleaning the sand out of the car and nursing Brenna through a cold were not great sacrifices to make for the gift of her joy that day. And yet if I could not learn that important lesson in loving, how could I give larger portions of myself?

The gift of teaching

Just as love requires sacrifice, so the gift of teaching has its own price and rewards. It would be easier if we could show love to our children by giving them expensive presents instead of ourselves. And it would be more convenient if we could teach our children by handing them over to professionals, by giving them a set of rules to follow, or by simply telling them what to do. But children learn by imitation. If we want to instill certain values in them, we must model those values in our own lives. Teaching, like love, requires giving ourselves.

Christ taught by example. He didn't ask his disciples to discuss what he told them or to commit his words to memory. He asked them to imitate his actions. In modeling servant-hood, Jesus got on his knees and washed his disciples' feet. Then he turned to them and said, "For I give you an example, that you also should do as I have done to you" (John 13:15).

The values that I would like to instill in my daughter were given to me by my parents: love, joy, peace, patience, kindness, goodness, faithfulness, gentleness, and self-control— the fruits of a Spirit-filled life (Gal. 5:22). If Brenna doesn't see those values reflected in my life, how can I expect her to learn them?

When my sister and I were small, there was a time when we fought like cats and dogs. My father asked why we always got into skirmishes. "You and Mommy do it, why can't we?" I retorted. My parents had no idea that their arguments had such an impact on us.

"The next time you see your mother and me fighting," said Dad, "I'll give you a dollar." At the first sound of dissension, I was there with my hand out. My father paid me, but only once—after that the fighting stopped between my parents and, in turn, between my sister and me.

While Christian parents are building love and faith into a child, they are themselves under the tutelage of their heavenly Father. They learn just as their children do. "Be imitators of God, as beloved children" (Eph. 5:1). Walk in the light, says Paul, and try to learn what pleases the Lord (Eph. 5:10). If we obey God's commandments out of love, our children are more likely to respond positively to our instructions.

When a child loves his parents, he naturally wants to please them. As soon as Brenna was aware of her own accomplishments, she looked to us for praise. When she first stood on shaky legs, when she first climbed a flight of stairs, her face was radiant. We smiled back and she beamed. Later we clapped and shouted, "Yea, Brenna!" She quickly learned to applaud for herself. To see her celebrate every time she conquered a milestone of learning gave us a tremendous thrill; there can be no greater reward for teaching.

The gift of discipline

Just as love requires sacrifice and teaching takes time, discipline too has its price: it hurts. Pediatricians, psychologists, and sociologists have written volumes on discipline. There are many different schools of thought, but generally the pendulum has swung toward permissiveness. In a society that teaches, "do it if it feels good," parents understandably shy away from disciplining their children. It doesn't feel good, so they don't do it.

Brenna was two months old when we had to suffer through the inevitable "bedtime crisis." When a baby begins to understand that going to bed means the end of play and companionship, he cries to make his parents come back. Parents have a choice: they can pick the baby up to quiet him, which encourages him to demand their constant presence, or they can be firm and let the baby cry himself to sleep. The crying can last several hours the first night; it gradually diminishes until the baby goes to bed without crying at all.

I explained the theory to Larry as Brenna's piercing cries echoed throughout the house. "I can't stand it," he said. "I love her. It hurts me to hear her cry. Do we have to do this?"

"Yes," I said firmly. Her cries tugged at my heart too. As a child, I had always thought my parents relished disciplining me. From my point of view, they seemed to be tyrants doling out punishment with a vengeance. I never realized until now that it might be hurting them deeply to see me suffer, that they were acutely aware of all my unhappiness.

Brenna was feeling the pain of rejection as we refused to go to her. Someday she would understand that we weren't rejecting her: we were loving her in a different way. As she discovered a new facet of our love for her, we explored our

65

own mixed emotions about exercising authority. How would this change our relationship? Would she resent our firmness?

Brenna's crying only lasted 20 minutes, though it seemed much, much longer. The next morning Larry and I rushed into her room and picked her up as soon as she started to wake. We both looked at each other and said at the same time, "I want to tell her that I'm sorry, that I still love her." As for Brenna, she was refreshed from a good night's sleep and acted as if nothing had happened.

After a few nights Brenna went to sleep without crying at all. The battle of wills had been resolved—until the next time. The next time came when Brenna learned to crawl. Until she was six months old, I used to spread her toys out on a blanket and she would be content to stay there. When she became mobile, she lost interest in her toys. The blanket, which once circumscribed her world, soon became a postage stamp in the vastness of new uncharted territory she yearned to explore. She became fascinated with big toys: furniture, leafy plants, and lamps.

A new word entered her vocabulary—no! I said no for the first time when she tugged on the fronds of a spider plant. She stopped and looked at me, then retreated. When I turned my back, she reached for the plant again. This process was repeated several times. I became more insistent, "Brenna, when Mommy says no, she means no." Those were words for me to hear. They didn't make sense to her. Finally I discovered that the only way to deter Brenna was to slap her hand hard enough to hurt her. I dreaded doing this; so did Larry.

He cringed when I suggested it. One day Brenna started to put a pebble down her throat and there was no time for a lengthy explanation or gentle reasoning. Larry had to yank it out of her mouth and slap her to warn her against doing it again. When the danger was real enough, we knew we had to hurt her to keep her from hurting herself.

Still, it didn't feel good. Love is complex. It has its soft side—cuddling and showing affection—and it has its hard side—establishing boundaries of behavior and punishing transgressions. We wanted Brenna to grow up knowing that love involves responsibility as well as freedom, sacrifice as well as indulgence because someday she would have to discipline herself.

The gift of forgiveness

Even though parents may be effective disciplinarians and children may be generally obedient, things still go wrong. We all make mistakes. The only way we can reconcile the imperfection in our lives is to forgive. "Be kind to one another, tenderhearted, forgiving one another as God in Christ forgave you" (Eph. 4:32).

A large part of parental giving involves forgiving. "How many times should you forgive?" Jesus was asked. "Seventy times seven," he replied. Parents understand the meaning of these words better than anyone else. It is pointless to count when the baby smears peanut butter and jelly in his hair for the umpteenth time, when the toilet paper is unrolled throughout the house, when the living room lamp crashes to the floor.

As children grow older, their thoughtlessness and willful defiance result in more serious consequences, often bringing their parents pain that seems impossible to bear. A rebellious teenager runs away, another takes drugs and drifts into crime. . . . "Seventy times seven," said Jesus.

When we think of how much our children can hurt us and how difficult it is to forgive their most heinous crimes, we would do well to consider how completely our heavenly Father forgives us. "For thou hast cast all my sins behind thy back" (Isa. 38:17). God forgives and forgets, giving us a new future with fresh possibilities.

There may be times when our children can hurt us beyond our power to forgive. A Christian parent turns to God for strength, relying on his promise: "My grace is sufficient for you, for my power is made perfect in weakness" (2 Cor. 12:9).

Our whole Christian sojourn is spent in that process: perfecting power in weakness. As children of God we are born with new natures, turning from pride to humility, recognizing our complete dependence on God. We are told to lay down our lives for others, to lose ourselves in giving and serving.

"For even the Son of Man did not come to be served, but to serve, and to give his life a ransom for many" (Mark 10:45 NASB). Charles Swindoll, in his book *Improving Your Serve: The Art of Unselfish Living* (Word, 1981), is disturbed by the fact that modern Christians, caught up in looking out for number one, have lost sight of who they are. He reminds us that we are called, like Christ, to adopt a life-style of servanthood.

If we are indeed called to be servants, not superstars, then parenthood is a natural training ground for developing the art of unselfish living. "Let each of you regard one another as more important than himself," Paul admonishes (Phil. 2:3 NASB). To be perfectly honest with myself, I had to admit that I had never truly put another person first in my life until I became a mother. Then all my other little acts of giving in other relationships paled in comparison with the total commitment I had to make.

One day as I was rinsing out a diaper in the toilet (a thankless job that even Larry refused to do), I calculated that in

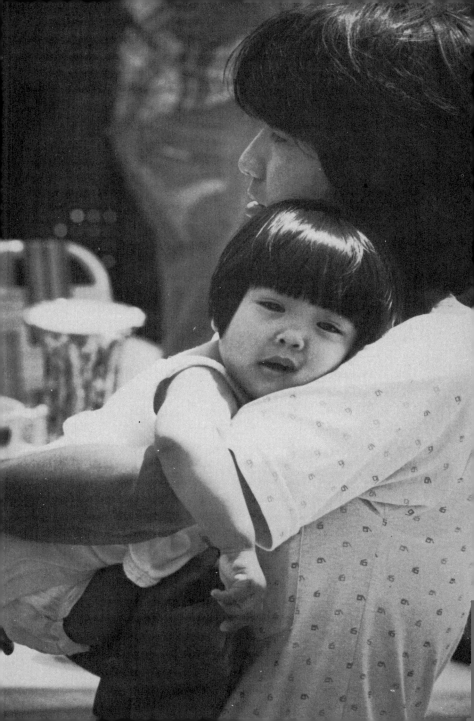

two and a half years I would have washed nearly 6000 diapers! Parenthood is an endless repetition of thankless chores, day after day.

If you don't think of yourself as a martyr or mother of the year, that realization can be daunting. But an amazing thing happens. As commitment grows, love grows, and you don't mind giving so totally of yourself.

Breastfeeding offers a good analogy. When a mother's milk comes in, she is sometimes afraid to nurse her baby too often for fear of "losing" her milk supply. Exactly the opposite is true: the more often the breasts are emptied, the more milk a mother has. If she stops nursing, her supply dries up completely.

In the same way, the more parents give, the greater is their capacity to give. They give and give and give until giving becomes a way of life. The giving and serving qualities that characterized Christ—compassion, tenderness, gentleness—begin to characterize them.

"We are never more godlike than when we give," writes Charles Swindoll. By developing a selfless life-style as parents, we grow closer to God. Something else happens to servants. They become genuine, transparent, absolutely honest with themselves and others. They become real.

To illustrate this, Swindoll uses an excerpt from a children's book, *The Velveteen Rabbit* by Margery Williams (Doubleday, 1958). The story is about a stuffed toy rabbit who comes to a child's nursery all shiny and new. He strikes up a conversation with the Skin Horse, a shabby, much-loved stuffed animal that has lived in the nursery for a long time.

The Skin Horse had lived longer in the nursery than any of the others. He was so old that his brown coat was bald in patches and showed the seams underneath, and most of the hairs in his tail had been pulled out to string bead necklaces. He was wise, for he had seen a long succession of mechanical toys arrive to boast and swagger, and by-and-by break their mainsprings and pass away, and he knew that they were only toys, and would never turn into anything else. For nursery magic is very strange and wonderful, and only those playthings that are old and wise and experienced like the Skin Horse understand all about it.

"What is REAL?" asked the Rabbit one day, when they were lying side by side near the nursery fender, before Nana came to tidy the room. "Does it mean having things that buzz inside you and a stick-out handle?"

"Real isn't how you're made," said the Skin Horse. "It's a thing that happens to you. When a child loves you for a long, long time, not just to play with, but REALLY loves you, then you become Real."

"Does it hurt?" asked the Rabbit.

"Sometimes," said the Skin Horse, for he was always truthful. "When you are Real you don't mind being hurt."

"Does it happen all at once, like being wound up," he asked, "or bit by bit?"

"It doesn't happen all at once," said the Skin Horse. "You become. It takes a long time. That's why it doesn't often happen to people who break easily, or have sharp edges, or who have to be carefully kept. Generally, by the time you are Real, most of your hair has been loved off, and your eyes drop out and you get loose in the joints and very shabby. But these things don't matter at all, because once you are real you can't be ugly, except to people who don't understand."

6

A Time to Receive

Learning what our children have to teach

In spite of the strain of becoming new parents, Larry and I were amazed by how much more Brenna gave us than we gave her. When we received God's gift of her presence in our lives, we could not begin to comprehend the blessings that she would bring. "Give, and it will be given to you," said Jesus, "good measure, pressed down, shaken together, running over, will be put into your lap" (Luke 6:38).

Larry came to bed late one night as I was drifting off to sleep. Gently he nudged me awake and put his arms around me. "Thank you for my daughter," he whispered. "Thank you. Thank you."

He had been standing by Brenna's crib watching her sleep. He still could not get over the beauty of her face—the delicate features, the long, feathery lashes, and the warm pink glow of her skin. I understood how he felt because I often stood by her crib gazing at her too.

"Why are you thanking me? She's half you," I said.

"I know." He thought a minute, then he smiled. "But she's all you under her diaper!"

Who was this child of ours? Was she simply an extension of us, an amalgam of our genes and personality traits? Certainly everyone was quick to tell us that my daughter's smile resembled mine, that her large, expectant eyes came from her father. It was flattering to see how similar she was to us, but I was more fascinated by Brenna's uniqueness.

All babies are born with blue eyes. Gradually, as pigment is added, their eye color may change to brown or green or hazel. I always expected my baby's eyes to be brown like mine, so I was surprised when Brenna's eyes did not turn dark. After six months I could see flecks of brown in her eyes, but there were also flecks of green and blue like Larry's. Brenna's eyes were an exact mixture of ours, a color wholly different than either Larry's or mine.

When I held Brenna up to the mirror, studying our resemblance, I was absolutely amazed. She did not look like a child of mine with those strange eyes. It was a small thing. But in that moment I sensed the beginning of many things that would surprise me as I unraveled the mystery of my daughter. Brenna was her own person, a separate being—a synthesis of Larry and me and something more.

I felt just as excited and apprehensive as she did when she began to discover that she had a unique identity, separate from us. The newborn is so completely absorbed in his parents that he knows no existence without them; it is equally difficult for parents to realize that their children aren't simply miniature versions of themselves. "Our children are part of us, and we constantly project our expectations onto them," says Angela McBride in *The Growth and Development of Mothers* (Harper & Row, 1973).

Even in giving, the seemingly selfless part of parenthood,

73

we can be self-serving. Giving puts us on the offensive. It allows us control. Receiving requires handing over that control to someone else. An eight-month-old baby resents having things being done to him; he wants to do. Instead of allowing his mother and father to feed him, he insists on feeding himself. To emphasize his independence he gets great satisfaction from offering his parents a part of the meal. This reversal of roles is a necessary part of growth and self-awareness. When our children are ready to give, we must be willing to receive.

In order to receive a gift, our hands must be empty. In order to receive a child, our hearts and minds must be open, creating what Henri Nouwen calls "a free and friendly space." In *Reaching Out* (Doubleday, 1975), the Dutch theologian writes, "Children are strangers whom we have to get to know. They have their own style, their own rhythm and their own capacities for good and evil. They cannot be explained by looking at their parents. . . . Children carry a promise with them, a hidden treasure that has to be led out into the open through education (*e* = out, *ducere* = to lead) in a hospitable home."

When Nouwen speaks of hidden treasure, he is referring to a child's innate gifts: abilities, talents, and skills that are gradually revealed in a nurturing atmosphere. But children come bearing other gifts as well—hidden treasure sent from our heavenly Father especially for parents.

"Whoever receives this child in my name receives me," said Jesus, "and whoever receives me receives him who sent me" (Luke 9:48). Christ came to earth as an infant, carrying a promise. As his mother nursed him, she must have pondered the meaning of his name: "God with us." Could it be that God's gift to humankind was God himself?

The miracle is not that this happened once, but that it continues to occur every time a child is born. "Whoever receives this child in my name receives me. . . ." This child: any child, every child. Whoever: parents, grandparents, teachers, and caregivers. All of us have the potential to discover who God is by uncovering a child's hidden treasure.

Why does God choose to reveal himself this way? Because we learn by imitation. Jesus said, "Unless you turn and become like children, you will never enter the kingdom of heaven" (Matt. 18:3). Just as we give our children gifts to help them grow, so God has given us the gift of children to instill Christ-like qualities in us.

What are the qualities we are meant to imitate in our children? I want to focus on just a few: enthusiasm, teachableness, trustfulness, an appreciation of the present, and a keen sense of wonder. There are many more. Every parent is familiar with these childlike characteristics, but they may not recognize them as Christ-like.

Enthusiasm

As soon as Brenna sees her father's face at the door when he comes home in the evening, her eyes grow bright like light bulbs, she kicks her feet together, and she bounces up and down in her high chair. That's enthusiasm. Children have a marvelous capacity for celebration and joy. They feel intensely, and they express their emotions with complete abandon.

Adults are amazed by this. We go through life with stiff upper lips, jaded, weary, lukewarm. It never occurs to us that indifference is an abomination to God. "Because you are lukewarm, and neither cold nor hot, I will spew you out of my mouth" (Rev. 3:16).

A story in second Samuel illustrates this point. During the reign of Saul, the Philistines captured the ark of God, the symbol of God's covenant with the Israelites. When David

became king, the Lord allowed him to bring back the ark. David led his people in a jubilant procession to recover the shrine. As the procession returned to Jerusalem, David's wife, Michal, saw her husband dancing in the street and leaping with joy. She was appalled. "How could you make such a fool of yourself?" she chided him. "You are a king, not a servant."

David was unashamed. "It was before the Lord," he said, ". . . and I will make merry before the Lord." David's dance was a prayer of praise for God's goodness. God was not offended by David's uninhibited outburst of praise, but he was greatly angered by Michal's lukewarm attitude. As a result, he cursed her: she remained childless until the day of her death.

Many modern couples, concerned with their own dignity and well-ordered life-style, have no room for children in their lives. For them choosing to remain childless is a blessing, not a curse. They cannot bear the unbridled enthusiasm of kids, their unpredictability and wanton energy. Sometimes parents can't bear it either.

Children are like little balls of energy. Their activity level is so intense that they can burn out the most easygoing parents. But that enthusiasm, which can be so exhausting and trying at times, is the same quality that infuses their lives with warmth and light. It invigorates parents and shakes them out of their dull routines. Without that spark of energy, they would drift into dignified, well-ordered indifference.

Teachableness

Children have a way of making us embrace rather than shrink away from what life has to offer. Their enthusiastic attitudes, which hurl them headlong into activity, also send them seeking into the unknown, always reaching beyond themselves. A child's teachableness is another quality that God would have us emulate.

During the first two years of life, an infant grows and develops rapidly. At birth he is conscious only of himself; he is the center of his own world. Gradually, as his intelligence unfolds, he realizes that he is part of a much larger universe. The Swiss child psychologist Jean Piaget calls this process a "miniature Copernican revolution" after the 15th century astronomer who discovered that the sun and other planets do not revolve around the earth as people once believed.

In *The Origins of Intelligence in Children* (W. W. Norton, 1963), Piaget describes how a child's mind develops. Babies learn, he says, by ceaseless exploration and experimentation. An infant may stumble upon a new sensory-motor activity by accident. Then he deliberately repeats the action again and again until he has mastered it. One action leads to another; each stage of development becomes a springboard for further development.

Babies are so driven in their desire to learn that they fill every waking hour testing, examining, and assimilating new knowledge. Jim Thorpe, a four-star athlete, once tried to imitate a baby's every move in a single day. After four hours he collapsed from exhaustion while the baby continued for four more hours!

Before Brenna could crawl, she had to teach herself to push up on her hands and knees. For weeks we heard her in her crib trying to perfect this maneuver. Each "umph" was followed by a "flop." Finally she was strong enough to rock back and forth in a crawling position. It took several more weeks to learn to move her arms and legs in unison so that she could propel herself forward.

Once she was mobile, the first thing she did was crawl

pell-mell into a wall. She kept butting her head against the obstacle, trying to plow right through it. After a while she learned that by putting her hands up against it, she could turn herself around and start crawling in the opposite direction.

Brenna did not seem to know the meaning of the word *failure*. She was frustrated at times, but she learned from her mistakes and kept trying until she accomplished her goal. It never occurred to her to give up. Driven by a compulsion to reach out and stretch herself, she continued to broaden her horizons.

All of a Christian's endeavors should be characterized by that kind of wholehearted effort. "Seek, and you will find," Jesus promised. "Knock, and it will be opened to you" (Matt. 7:7). Most Christians only knock once. The door of salvation swings open and they think they have arrived. A child would not be content to stop there. His curiosity would lead him to open one door after another discovering more and more of God's promises. If we don't maintain a seeking mind, we cannot grow spiritually and be all that God wants us to be.

Trustfulness

Reaching out requires faith. When Jesus appeared to the disciples walking on the Sea of Galilee, they thought they were seeing a ghost. He assured them there was nothing to fear. "Lord, if it is you," Peter said, "bid me come to you on the water." At Christ's bidding, Peter got out of the boat and walked to him. Suddenly Peter became aware of the wind and waves. "Lord, save me," he cried out as he began to sink. Jesus stretched out his hand and saved Peter, saying, "O man of little faith, why did you doubt?" (Matt. 14: 26-31).

79

Adults do not come easily to faith because they have lost their ability to trust. Anyone who has seen a baby learn to walk has witnessed faith in action. A one-year-old takes his first unsupported steps staggering through space to his father's arms. His confidence is not in himself, but in his father. This is the kind of absolute trust that Christ asked of Peter, and he also asks it of us. In order to follow Christ we have to rediscover in ourselves that childlike quality of trust.

For many years my mother taught Sunday school at a children's hospital. One Sunday she told the story of the parents who brought their babies to Jesus for his blessing. When the disciples pushed the bothersome parents away, the Lord rebuked them. "Let the children come to me," he said, lifting them up into his arms. My mother explained that Jesus is never too busy to care for little ones; each child is precious to him.

As the children were being wheeled back to their rooms that Sunday, a three-year-old came up to my mother and looked up at her with shy, quiet eyes. Without saying a word, he took her hand and led her down the corridor to the leukemia ward.

Most of the rooms were filled with toys, and many had an adult bed where parents slept overnight. But this toddler's room was bare. There were only two things in his closet: a tiny pair of cowboy boots and a picture that he had colored in Sunday school. The picture of Jesus leading a small boy by the hand was taped to his closet door. As he pointed to it, a big smile spread across his face.

"What a beautiful picture," my mother said. "Thank you so much for showing it to me."

This little boy, alone in the world and dying of cancer, knew that Jesus loved him. Jesus was as real to him as any parent or friend. There was nothing mysterious to him about falling in love, about needing comfort and support. He gave himself wholeheartedly to Christ, as children do to anyone they love.

God never betrays our trust. If we doubt his promises, he tells us to test them. "Bring the full tithes into the storehouse, that there may be food in my house; and thereby put me to the test, says the Lord of hosts, if I will not open the windows of heaven for you and pour down for you an overflowing blessing" (Mal. 3:10). Christians who have walked with the Lord for years can testify from experience to God's faithfulness.

An appreciation of the present

If we trust God to provide for our needs, then we have no reason to worry about tomorrow or to feel burdened about the past. Christ tells us to live for today. He taught us to pray for our daily bread one day at a time. Another Christlike quality that our children model for us is an appreciation of the present.

I thought about this many times when I was nursing Brenna. Breast-feeding or bottle-feeding offers a quiet, intimate exchange between parent and infant. According to pediatrician Berry Brazelton, these moments are "solid gold" for a baby. With his physical and emotional needs satisfied, the infant basks in contentment.

These can be golden moments for moms too, but sometimes my mind would wander, racing ahead to make plans for that evening or mulling over something that had happened days before. Meanwhile Brenna lightly stroked my breast or fiddled with a strand of my hair, trying to draw me close to share the pleasurable moment at hand.

To babies, moments in the day are like the beads of a necklace: they examine each bead individually, fully exploring every facet of one before moving on to another. Young children look at days this same way. Their three-month summer break from school seems to last forever because each carefree day is packed with adventure and new experiences.

"This is the day which the Lord has made," David sang, "let us rejoice and be glad in it" (Ps. 118:24). What is life, after all, but a series of moments and days? How much we miss if we don't live each to the fullest!

A sense of wonder

Just as children celebrate the glory of a new day, they rejoice in all of God's creation. In their eyes everything is wonderful, marvelous, and new. William Blake captures a child's sense of wonder in his poem "Auguries of Innocence":

To see a world in a grain of sand,
And a heaven in a wild flower;
Hold infinity in the palm of your hand,
And eternity in an hour.

I discovered this sense of wonder in my daughter as I watched her waken to the world around her. As Blake suggests, a child looks into the mystery of life by peering through the tiniest windows. One day I found Brenna sitting in our bedroom gazing very intently at nothing. Her brow was furrowed with concentration as she reached out and grabbed fistfuls of air. I couldn't figure out what she was doing. As I drew closer, I could see that she was trying to catch floating particles of dust illuminated by the sunlight!

Things that were commonplace to me enthralled Brenna.

She could spend hours tracing shadows on the wall and studying the pattern on a Sunmaid raisin box. She was amazed the first time I set her on the kitchen floor instead of the carpeted living room. She looked at the brick pattern in the tile, then she ran her hand over the floor and slapped it with her palm. The kitchen floor felt hard and smooth, not furry like the carpet.

Larry and I began to look for opportunities to show Brenna something new just to see her reaction. The first time she rode in a stroller, or on the back of our bikes, or was pushed in a swing, she giggled hilariously and squealed with delight. Her joy doubled and tripled our pleasure, making a simple outing an event we long remembered.

Why do adults lose their sense of wonder and joy of discovery? With Solomon we moan, "There's nothing new under the sun." Arthur Gordon in *A Touch Of Wonder* (Fleming H. Revell, 1974) suggests a very practical way that we can fall in love with life again. "I learned that sometimes when you're feeling jaded or blasé, you can revive your sense of wonder by saying to yourself: *Suppose this sunset, this moonrise, this symphony, this buttered toast, this sleeping child, this flag against the sky . . . suppose you would never experience these things again!* Few things are commonplace in themselves. It's our reaction to them that grows dull as we move forward through the years."

There is another way we can activate our sense of wonder. Again, we'll take our cue from children. It was very disconcerting to me when Brenna began arching her back and throwing her head back while sitting on my lap. We called her our "laid-back" baby for a while. Later I learned that this was normal. Babies like to look at the world upside down to gain a different perspective, which is all part of their visual experimenting. We need constantly to refresh our vision by looking at things in a new way—whether it be an object, an opportunity, or a relationship.

When the prophet Isaiah wanted to impress the Israelites with the Lord's greatness, he described God from a unique perspective. God's chosen people had become proud and rebellious when Isaiah addressed them; they had lost their fear of the Lord. To rekindle that reverence, Isaiah reminds them of just how small and insignificant they appear to the Creator of the universe.

The prophet asks: "Who has measured the waters in the hollow of his hand and marked off the heavens with a span, enclosed the dust of the earth in a measure and weighed the mountains in scales and the hills in a balance? . . . Behold, the nations are like a drop from a bucket, and are accounted as the dust on the scales; behold, he takes up the isles like fine dust" (Isa. 40:12, 15).

Isaiah is giving us a child's-eye view of God. This passage reminds me of the times when Brenna plays at my feet while I'm doing the dishes. Suddenly I feel her little arms clinging to my legs. She pulls herself up and burrows her head between my knees, smiling up at me. I must appear to be a colossus, towering so far above her. To small children the whole world appears gigantic, awesome.

Few of us view God from this perspective with a sense of wonder and awe. If we did, we would be spellbound by life's possibilities, because this same all-powerful Creator cares intimately for each of us. "Even the hairs of your head are all numbered," says Jesus (Matt. 10:30). The Almighty is a God of grace and a Father of infinite love. The blessings he wants to give us are beyond anything we could imagine.

Just as I reach down to Brenna and give her a cuddle when she hugs my knees, God reaches down from his lofty height to show his love for us. That love is available every time we seek it; a child would not hesitate to ask.

Our children's ways may seem strange to us. They don't always behave as we expect them to or say the things we think they should. As Henri Nouwen says, they are strangers whom we have to get to know. As they grow and change, we are bound to change too, which can be unsettling or challenging.

Perhaps that's part of the plan. "Do not neglect to show hospitality to strangers, for thereby some have entertained angels unawares" (Heb. 13:2). Our children are heavenly messengers sent to us for a purpose. Our task is to receive them with love and learn what they have to teach.

7

A Time to Laugh

Looking at
the lighter side of life

When Brenna hugs my knees, begging to be held, I usually give her a quick cuddle and send her on her way. But sometimes that is not enough. As soon as she settles on my hip, she often likes to stay there. She inevitably does this in the evening when I am rushing around the kitchen trying to get dinner on the table.

One time while Brenna balanced on my hip, I was hurrying to put the kettle on, stir the soup, and set the table. With my free hand I jerked open a kitchen drawer and sent it flying onto the floor.

I was furious. Mason jar lids, plastic forks, measuring spoons, kitchen gadgets, and a conglomeration of odds and ends were strewn everywhere. "Brenna Lee!" I shouted. "Look what you made Mommy do. What a mess!"

Brenna looked at me uncomprehendingly, not hurt by my outburst, but puzzled. As I got down on my hands and knees to pick up the contents of the junk drawer, I watched Brenna out of the corner of my eye. I was afraid that she would have a field day scattering everything throughout the house.

But that is not at all what she did. Very fastidiously, she picked up a single toothpick, handed it to me, and smiled. I didn't know whether to laugh or cry. All the anger and tension bottled up inside me suddenly disappeared.

I felt very foolish getting so uptight over such a little thing. Brenna handed me another toothpick and another and another, proud of herself and wanting to please me. To her, picking up toothpicks was an interesting pursuit. She'd just as soon do that as help stir the soup.

Whenever I became frustrated or took the business of living too seriously, Brenna reminded me of how simple life was meant to be and how complicated adults can make it. A baby brings laughter into the house and the art of looking at the lighter side of things.

Again and again Brenna rescued Larry and me from the tensions that can so easily tie us in knots. Once we were going to a dinner party. We were late, and everything that could go wrong, did. As we drove toward the freeway, Larry noticed that the gas tank was nearly empty. That was the last straw.

"Why didn't you fill the tank?" he asked.

"*You* drove the car last."

"Do you have any cash?"

I checked through my pockets and couldn't find a penny.

Larry threw up his hands. "We'll never find a station that takes credit cards at this time of night!"

Our tempers were mounting when we heard a tiny voice from the backseat echo, "Uh-oh." Uh-oh was Brenna's first word, and she had a knack for saying it at the most appropriate times.

Exasperated, I turned around and glared at her. "Brennn-na!" I wasn't in the mood for jokes, intended or unintended.

Brenna was oblivious to the gathering storm. She giggled, relishing our attention. "Uh-oh, uh-oh, uh-oh," she continued nonstop like a broken record.

Larry and I tried to keep straight faces, but we couldn't. We both broke out laughing, which encouraged Brenna to start a new round of uh-ohs. The crisis of the gas tank which had loomed so large moments before now didn't seem to matter anymore. What mattered was our laughter and having a good time together.

We never felt closer as a family than when we laughed together. And Brenna loved playing the master of ceremonies. Just as her social smile as an infant had set off a chain reaction of grins, her laughter also had a magical appeal. We couldn't help laughing at her and with her.

We take Brenna's laughing for granted now, but the ability to laugh, like all of her achievements, has evolved slowly over time. The smile of a newborn, a slight upward turn of the mouth, is caused by a discharge of tension; it is more of a reflex than a response. As the infant begins to react to stimulation outside himself, the drowsy grimace gives way to an alert, open-eyed grin. By four or five months, a baby's chuckling and gurgling erupt into full-blown laughter.

I will never forget the first time I heard Brenna laugh out loud. "Ssssh!" Larry motioned for me to be quiet and to stand outside our bedroom door. While I watched, he stuck out his tongue and blew a raspberry at Brenna. She grinned from ear to ear, her eyes crinkling with delight. Then she burst into loud, rolling laughter that almost shook her out of her infant chair.

Larry and I looked at each other, astonished. Brenna's funny pumpkin face and hilarious belly laugh were so extra-

ordinary that we tried to get her to laugh again. The raspberry trick was good for a couple more times, then she tired of it. Her laughter disappeared for several weeks.

No matter how hard Larry tried—making funny faces and goofy sounds—he couldn't get her to laugh. Our friends tried too. They bounced her on their knees, waved their arms, and puckered their lips. I was amazed by how foolishly people would act just to make a tiny baby giggle. Finally a seasoned grandfather's Donald Duck imitation tickled Brenna so much that she burst out laughing again.

We all had so much fun trying to get Brenna to laugh that I began to wonder why adults don't laugh more often. Is laughter something that our children have to teach us? We smile when we are amused. We chuckle at jokes. But how often do we really let go and roar with laughter?

"Unless you turn and become like children, you will never enter the kingdom of heaven" (Matt. 18:3). One of the secrets of becoming more childlike is learning to laugh. Laughter is a brimming over of exuberance: it lights up our lives and lightens our burdens.

Babies quickly learn how to amuse their parents. When Brenna discovered tricks that made us laugh, she loved performing them over and over again. Of course we encouraged her by having her repeat them in front of friends. As soon as she had an audience, she launched into a carefully rehearsed routine that left us all in stitches.

At the age of a year, her routine went something like this. First she clicked her tongue against the roof of her mouth. We clicked back, repeating and modulating the sound into a kind of musical conversation. She followed this by pulling up her shirt and pointing to her belly button. As she pushed it in, we yelled, "Beep!" which made Brenna drop her shirt and clap, grinning with delight. Her finale was a sideways wave good-bye.

Several times Brenna made us laugh so hard that tears streamed down our faces. At 13 months, her temper started to show. If she didn't get what she wanted, she would tense up, clenching her fists and shaking all over. To discourage this, we laughed off her tantrums. When she realized this was a way to amuse us, she turned it into a joke.

One evening after dinner, she got our attention and began to mimic a tantrum. She held her breath, turning red, then let go with gales of laughter, which cracked us up. The more we laughed, the tighter she clenched her fists. She looked like a cartoon character with steam hissing out of her ears, about to explode. Larry and I nearly split our sides with laughter. We finally had to stop laughing because it hurt so much.

When Brenna made us laugh that hard, we could actually feel the tensions of the day drain away. It relaxed us; we felt renewed psychologically and physically. Aside from the obvious value of looking at the lighter side of life and the bonding benefits of having a good time together, laughter has real physical benefits. Studies have shown that it relieves stress, acting as a "safety valve" for pent-up nervous energy. Laughter *may be* the best medicine.

Laughter also has value for children. As I mentioned in the previous chapter, a baby is driven to explore and expand his horizons. Laughter is one of the mechanisms he uses to cope with the unknown. It frees him to go beyond himself.

How does a child use laughter to do this? Peek-a-boo was the earliest game that made Brenna laugh. I would cover my face with a cloth, then quickly pull it away. The novelty excited Brenna, but she was also frightened because she was not sure where I had gone. Suddenly my face reappeared. She laughed as her tension was released.

As she became more confident and recognized that my disappearance was just a game, she wanted to play too. She took the cloth and covered her face, this time hiding from me. By playing a game, Brenna was acting out and learning to cope with the real fear of being separated from me.

Like all babies, Brenna enjoyed discovering and mastering new situations. In familiar surroundings with Larry or me nearby, she felt secure enough to explore what would otherwise seem threatening. By releasing her tension in a positive way through laughter she could continue to approach a novel experience until she understood it.

Novelty seeking is a kind of problem solving. A child acquires certain concepts of the world from his experience. When he encounters a new event that doesn't fit that concept, he has to stretch the concept to assimilate the new experience. By adding his knowledge to what he already knows, he expands his intelligence and broadens his view of the world.

This can be a serious pursuit or a humorous one. If a child

is in a playful mood, making sense of incongruities can be fun. "Incongruity is at the core of all humor experiences," says Paul McGhee in *Humor: Its Origin and Development* (W. H. Freeman & Co., 1979). We laugh when we encounter something that is unexpected, illogical, exaggerated, or absurd.

Even though an infant begins to laugh at four or five months (from pleasure, recognition, or amusement), his sense of humor does not develop until the first half of the second year.

McGhee points out that children go through different stages of humor. They begin by appreciating small incongruities in the real world, then go on to create their own incongruities. For example, they often pretend to use one object as if it were another. At two and three they play with language, mislabeling objects and making up nonsense words. Preschoolers develop conceptual humor, laughing at the incongruous appearance of things, like an elephant in a tree. By seven or eight, children understand multiple meanings of words, and they enjoy jokes, puns, and riddles. Their humor gradually becomes more subtle and complex, and they develop an appreciation for irony, satire, and paradox.

But all this begins in a very simple way, so simple that parents can easily overlook their baby's first humorous experience. For Brenna it came at 14 months when she was learning to nod her head yes and shake her head no. Larry teased her by nodding his head up and down, shaking it from side to side, then rotating it round and round. Brenna saw the nonsense of that and thought it was hilarious.

Children create their own humorous situations during the latter half of their second year. They can't do this until they are able to think symbolically, representing objects with mental pictures in their memory. Brenna would giggle to herself as she combed her hair with a pencil. She had a mental picture of what a real comb looked like and it amused her to imagine using a pencil like a comb.

As she developed language skills, she would enjoy using the incorrect word for an object just to show that she had mastered the correct word. In name-change humor, toddlers find it funny to call a dog a cat, an ear an eye, a bird a cow.

Russian children's writer Koreii Chukovsky tells the story of his two-year-old daughter's first joke in his book *From Two to Five* (U. of California, 1963). She was fascinated with animal sounds and felt a great sense of pride to report that dogs bark and cats miaow. One day she ran to her father with a big smile on her face and shouted, "Daddy, 'oggie miaow!"

Chukovsky's first reaction was to correct her. "No," he said, "the doggie bow-wows." Then he saw the joke and joined in her game: "And the rooster miaows!" She laughed at this and went away merrily thinking up other mismatching animal sounds. Her father's approval, which at first she doubted, gave her the freedom to "topsy-turvy the world" according to her whim.

To adults this fantasy play may seem meaningless and a waste of time. But children stretch themselves by exploring the impossible as well as the possible. For generations children have loved nursery rhymes and folk tales based on absurdities and nonsense. Eggs don't sit on walls, cats don't fiddle, and dishes don't run away with spoons. But it's fun to imagine they might.

When Brenna was a year and a half, we took her to her first movie, *The Great Muppet Caper*. The star of the movie is Miss Piggy who appears as a fashion model, complete with a coiffured hairdo and pearls. When Miss Piggy made her dramatic debut, Brenna jumped up and down and shrieked with laughter. She was used to seeing pigs as barnyard animals in her storybooks; to see one made up like that was novel and very funny.

At first Larry and I were absorbed in watching Brenna enjoy the movie, but after a while we were laughing just as hard as she was. At one point a well-to-do couple in formal dress are talking over the dinner table about how boring and uneventful life is when suddenly they hear a clatter outside. "It's just a pig climbing up the side of the house, dear," the husband informs his wife. Within minutes their calm, cloistered existence is turned upside down by the hilarious antics of Miss Piggy and Kermit the Frog. I'm sure the adults in the audience got the message.

As we grow older, we become mechanical in our behavior, conforming to expectations and the rules we impose on ourselves; our view of the world becomes smaller and smaller. Sometimes we cling so stubbornly to our limited concept of reality that we need to be shaken free by encountering the incongruous and unexpected.

Fantasy serves the same purpose for adults as it does for children: it helps us look at life in a new and novel way. It keeps us creative, flexible, spontaneous, and open-minded.

We can encourage or discourage playfulness in our children. Chukovsky's experience with his daughter emphasizes how important parents' reactions are to the budding humorist. If parents ignore a child's jokes and fantasy play or if they dismiss it as silly and not worthwhile, the child's enjoyment of humor is likely to diminish. If, on the other hand, parents respond positively and affectionately to a child's humorous inventions, he will learn to amuse himself that way and seek opportunities to share his jokes with others.

As two new parents proudly pointed to their baby in a hospital nursery, they were bubbling with excitement. "He's going to be a great kid," the father told me. "But he looks so serious. I keep telling him to perk up. Life is fun!" Those parents will undoubtedly nurture warmth and humor in their son, and he in turn will brighten other lives with laughter.

Life *is* fun, but it is also complex and it doesn't always make sense. Fostering a sense of humor in our children allows them not only to revel in life, but also to cope with conflict and to broaden their perspectives. For Christian parents, there is an even more compelling reason to encourage laughter—God has a sense of humor.

"There is laughter and gaiety in the heart of God," says Elton Trueblood. How does he know? Because Christ had a sense of humor. In *The Humor Of Christ* (Harper & Row, 1964), the distinguished theologian challenges the conventional stereotype of a Christ who is always somber and deadly serious. This is only part of the picture, he says. Jesus was a man of sorrows, but he was also a man of joys.

Unlike the religious leaders of the day, Jesus did not hold himself aloof from society. He was usually in the thick of things, surrounded by a crowd of rough fisherfolk, farmers, and tentmakers. His speech was plain and often blunt, unembroidered with pious phrases. He told jokes, and his audience must have laughed at his quick wit. Why then is the humorous aspect of Christ's teaching so neglected?

The fault is ours, says Trueblood. We assume that religion must be a serious business and that joking about it would be blasphemous. But humor can be profound and thought-provoking, revealing truths that would otherwise remain hidden. It is not surprising that children, who enjoy laughing so much, readily respond to Christ's humor.

Trueblood admits that he would never have discovered the humorous side of Christ's teaching were it not for his four-year-old son. One day Trueblood was reading very seriously to his son from the seventh chapter of Matthew. The little boy burst out laughing when he heard Jesus ask the question: "How can you take a speck out of your brother's eye when there is a log in your own eye?" Because the child knew that a log could never fit in a human eye, he immediately recognized how incongruous the idea was.

From that moment on, Trueblood became acutely aware of Christ's wit and humor. He found that the parables are full of fanciful incongruities. Like children's rhymes, they are based on nonsense: casting pearls to swine, camels fitting through the eyes of needles, and figs growing from thistles. Jesus used absurd metaphors, says Trueblood, so that his listeners would remember the stories and realize the radical quality of his message.

Jesus' parables are meant to make us look at life in a totally new way, and if we take them seriously we are forced to change our lives dramatically. We are instructed to give up material wealth for spiritual values, to save our lives by losing them, to seek greatness through humility.

These commands fly in the face of what the world teaches, which is why the ways of God are so mysterious to us. To some they represent fantasy; to others they are the ultimate reality. "For the foolishness of God is wiser than men, and the weakness of God is stronger than men" (1 Cor. 1:25).

Although Christ used several types of humor to clarify his message, he most frequently used irony—pointing out vice or folly to public view. Irony is playful; it has none of the derisive or biting quality of sarcasm.

Jesus particularly enjoyed poking fun at the Pharisees in this way. In Matthew 23 he draws a picture of a fastidious Pharisee who takes elaborate pains to clean and polish the outside of his cup, while leaving the inside untouched and filthy. He strains what he is going to drink, and while carefully picking a gnat out of the liquid, he manages to swallow a whole camel, hump and all!

There is something of the Pharisee in each of us. We are the first to point out pretense in someone else, but the last to admit it in ourselves. Most of us lead double lives, rationalizing away or covering up the obvious contradictions between what we imagine ourselves to be and what we are.

A child is keenly aware of contradictions. With his innocent eye, he sees right through pretense and hypocrisy. To him it is laughable. Perhaps that is why Jesus said that children would clearly understand his teaching while wise men would be confused by it: "I thank thee, Father, Lord of heaven and earth, that thou hast hidden these things from the wise and understanding and revealed them to babes" (Matt. 11:25).

How, then, can we learn to laugh like children? Jesus gave some specific suggestions in the Beatitudes, a list of eight character traits that a Christian should strive for. J. B. Phillips translates the phrase "blessed are" as "how happy are." These attitudes offer the key to a happy life; two in particular apply to the gaiety of children.

"Blessed are the pure in heart," said Jesus, "for they shall see God" (Matt. 5:8). Children are unaffected and straightforward; they are not concerned with impressing other people and worrying about outward appearances. Perhaps that is part of the reason why adults don't laugh more often. Our lives are complicated and cluttered by unnecessary anxieties that don't allow us simply to be ourselves.

Children are pure in heart and humble in spirit. Humility is another virtue that Jesus extols. "Blessed are the poor in spirit, for theirs is the kingdom of heaven" (Matt. 5:3). We have all known people who appear to have everything—material well-being, professional success, perhaps fame—yet happiness eludes them. In their relentless drive toward success, somehow their spirits have been spent.

Children, on the other hand, are not puffed up by their own self-importance. Their happiness is not measured by what they have or what they achieve; their joy springs from a deep contentment within. They enjoy life simply for its own sake, and so they are free to celebrate it.

Children love to dance and sing. When Brenna is happy, she spins in circles and sings along with the radio, waving her arms and swinging her head from side to side. All little ones are gifted with music in their hearts. Babies adore the sound of rattles, clattering trinkets, and musical mobiles. They hum themselves to sleep and wake up cooing like birds singing a morning song.

Christians are supposed to express their joy at being alive in just the same way. "Sing to the Lord a new song, . . . let the saints rejoice in this honor and sing for joy on their beds" (Ps. 149:1, 5 NIV). A Christian who is

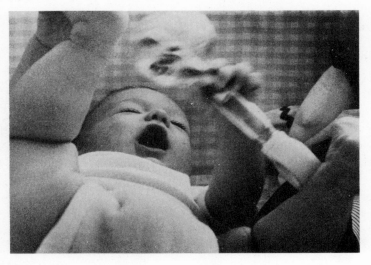

truly happy in the Lord has a song in his heart all day long, every day, not just in the sanctuary on Sunday.

Whenever I lose my ability to sing and laugh and celebrate life, I let my daughter lead me back to Happyland. According to Brenna's book *Mr. Happy* (Price/Stern/Sloan, 1971), Happyland is a country where everybody has smiles on their faces, even the animals and flowers.

It sounds fanciful, but Roger Hargreaves' description of Happyland is remarkably similar to the kingdom God envisioned for his children. "For you shall go out in joy, and be led forth in peace," Isaiah prophesied, "the mountains and the hills before you shall break forth into singing, and all the trees of the field shall clap their hands" (Isa. 55:12).

Mr. Happy, a round little man, is an inhabitant of Happyland. One day he comes across someone who looks just like him except he has a frown on his face. His name, of course, is Mr. Miserable.

"Why are you so miserable?" asks Mr. Happy.

"Because I am," says Mr. Miserable.

Mr. Happy takes Mr. Miserable home with him to Happyland. After a while, Mr. Miserable begins to notice a change. His mouth turns up at the corners, he smiles, he chuckles, and then he laughs—"a big booming hearty huge giant large enormous laugh."

Pretty soon Mr. Miserable and Mr. Happy are rolling on the ground with laughter. Everybody who sees them starts laughing too, even the birds in the trees.

"If you ever feel as miserable as Mr. Miserable used to," says Mr. Happy, "you know exactly what to do, don't you? Just turn your mouth up at the corners. Go on!"

8

A Time to Cry

Growing closer through tears

Laugh and the world laughs with you; cry and you cry alone. We loved laughing with Brenna and sharing her laughter with our friends; those were times of light. But as our love for one another grew, there also were times of darkness.

As we sped down the freeway one night toward the emergency clinic, I was reminded of that night many months ago when Larry and I had driven down the same road, excited and breathless, expecting the birth of our baby. Now our daughter lay in my arms, her cheeks flushed with fever.

My eyes were fixed on her tiny fingers resting in my hand. If they moved, even slightly, I felt relieved. Worry exaggerated my worst fears. I knew that high fevers could result in brain damage, even death. Was her illness serious? Larry drove on in silence. A sickening dread caught in our throats, preventing us from sharing our thoughts.

I brooded on my helplessness. There was nothing I could

do to relieve Brenna's suffering. Even though her little body nestled safely in my arms, she seemed far away, beyond my protection.

And Brenna. What was she thinking? She must have wondered, "Why doesn't Mommy stop my head from burning?" She was unable to anticipate an end to her suffering and unable to comprehend the reason for her pain.

Larry was practical and pragmatic. He had stripped Brenna down and bathed her to break her fever. It couldn't be serious, he assured me. Now he was bewildered. Why hadn't the treatment worked? What went wrong?

As we drove to the hospital, I knew this trip would not be our last. What frightened me was the power suffering had to alienate us, to lock us inside ourselves and isolate us from each other. If the solid foundation of our family could be so easily shaken, then how could we withstand the shock of childhood accidents that were bound to come?

Would Larry and I turn against each other in a crisis as so many parents do? "I told you never to take your eyes off her while she is riding her tricycle." "We never should have bought the tricycle. That was *your* idea."

How would we handle the emotional hurts Brenna would bring? If she drifted into trouble as a teenager, would we hurl accusations at one another, or would we silently harbor resentments that seethed beneath the surface of a fragile tranquility? I had heard stories of parental anxiety that spiraled into frustration and guilt, ending in bitter arguments and separation of family members. Could it happen to us?

Tears, our society teaches, are not to be shared. Pain should be hidden, glossed over, buried and forgotten. And so we cling to our anxieties secretly. We suffer alone. We have all said at some time: "No one really knows the depth of my sorrow. No one understands how I feel, not even those who are closest to me." We are too timid to reach out for help and too proud to accept help from others.

But Christians are called to compassion, to reach out to one another in sorrow, to be vulnerable and available—no matter how painful that may be, no matter what the cost. "Wanting to alleviate pain without sharing," writes Henri Nouwen, "is like wanting to save a child from a burning house without the risk of being hurt."

If we are unable or unwilling to take risks in our families, how can we reach out to a hurting world? As members of God's family, we are admonished to share our burdens. "If one member suffers," says Paul, "all suffer together" (1 Cor. 12:26). That kind of total sharing starts with individuals in our own families: husband and wife, parent and child.

I thought I was compassionate, until I became a parent. As a mother that emotion took on new meaning. In Aramaic, the language Jesus spoke, the word *compassion* comes from the root word "womb." I remembered the early weeks of motherhood when Brenna's cries made my uterus contract with concern. She seemed like an extension of my own body. If she was distressed, I felt distressed; if she slept fitfully, I could not sleep. I had never empathized with another human being so completely.

Compassion. Womb. I thought about that as I witnessed the birth of Susan's baby (she asked me to go with her to the hospital to take pictures). Susan and John are our closest friends. They were with us at the Malt Shop when Brenna was about to be born. I remembered Susan's excitement when we told her that our baby was on the way. As Brenna grew up, Susan had become a second mother to her.

A year later Susan was waiting for her own baby to arrive. She had taken natural childbirth classes and prepared herself for delivery just as I had. I reminded her of the words that had comforted me: "God will not let you be tempted beyond your strength." My delivery had been easy; just how easy I began to realize as I watched Susan in labor.

After an hour and a half of hard pushing, she was in excruciating pain. The baby was lodged in a posterior position and it could not be delivered naturally. The doctor told her that forceps would have to be used, but before the baby could be pulled free, he had to deaden the nerves in her back. The "saddle block" procedure, which should have taken five minutes, took nearly an hour. To Susan it must have seemed like an eternity.

Susan's cries pierced me to the center of my being. The empathy I felt for her was more than the way friends suffer together: it was much deeper and more real. I found myself imagining that she was my daughter; as a mother, I internalized her pain as if it were my own.

Christians have always struggled with the problem of pain. If God loves us, why does he let us suffer? Why does one human being suffer more than another? There is nothing good about suffering, says C. S. Lewis in *The Problem of Pain* (Macmillan, 1943); it is intrinsically evil. But good can come of it: the sufferer may learn submission to the will of God and compassion may be aroused in the spectator that leads to acts of mercy.

As a spectator, I could not fathom how God could use Susan's pain for her good. I was still asking why she had to endure it, why my delivery had been easy and hers so difficult, when in a miraculous moment her agony was transformed to joy. "Oh, she's so beautiful!" Susan whispered. As she feasted her eyes on her baby for the first time, Susan's euphoria was not any less than mine had been—in spite of the pain.

As mother and daughter smiled at one another and melted

103

into their silent oneness, Susan ceased to be a separate being. She and her baby had been one physically, now they would be emotionally one. The unfolding of that bonding process is no less mysterious than the inner workings of the womb.

Womb. Compassion. I realized, as I watched that new intimacy being born, that I was connected to my own daughter in the same way and that through her I was allowing myself to be connected to other human beings just as closely. The deep compassion that I felt for Susan sprang forth from a well of love that my daughter had aroused within me.

Compassion, Lewis said, leads to acts of mercy. The sufferer and spectator become one; love flows forth—invigorating, strengthening, healing. Without compassion, one human being cannot understand and enter into the pain of another. Without compassion, Christians cannot be comforters.

"Man is born to trouble," said Job. Because we live in an imperfect world, we are all subject to illness, accident, death, war, natural disasters, and injustice. God did not promise that Christians would be exempt from suffering. But because our heavenly Father is compassionate, he sent his Spirit, the Comforter, to help us in our pain. In turn Christians are expected to help others.

"Blessed be the God and Father of our Lord Jesus Christ, the Father of mercies and God of all comfort," writes Paul, "who comforts us in all our affliction, so that we may be able to comfort those who are in any affliction, with the comfort with which we ourselves are comforted by God" (2 Cor. 1:3-4).

To offer comfort is to offer more than compassion. The good Samaritan was moved with compassion when he saw a stranger badly beaten and left to die by the roadside. But he did more than merely identify with the man's pain; he

took steps to relieve it. He treated the man's wounds and took him to an inn where he could rest and recuperate.

Christian parents must be, above all else, comforters to their children—sharing their pain and helping to relieve it. We quickly learn to calm a crying infant with a bottle of milk or a cuddle, but how do we discern and offer comfort to the hidden cries of a teenager?

Adolescence is often the most painful stage of growing up. It certainly was for me. I remember coming home from a junior high dance, absolutely shattered. I had hovered in the shadows of the gym all evening, a tall, gawky teenager, hoping and praying that someone would ask me to dance. No one did. I was mortified.

My father met me at the door when I came home. He could have ignored the hurt in my eyes and whisked me off to bed where I would have cried myself to sleep. But he chose to share my pain. He listened patiently while I told him how miserable I felt. My suffering was just as real to him as it was to me.

"Life isn't fair," I sobbed.

Dad didn't minimize my heartache. "I never told you life was fair," he said. Then he told me about the humiliation and loneliness he had suffered while growing up. It helped just to know that I wasn't the only one who felt so painfully alone.

My father also had the benefit of an adult perspective. He had survived the emotional turmoil of adolescence and he knew that I would too. Before long, he told me, boys would be lined up at my door. He reminded me of the ugly duckling whose awkwardness only lasted a short time. Someday, my father promised, I would be a swan.

Then he took my hand and asked me to dance. As I glided across the living room in my father's arms, I felt very special. In the way he held me, in the love reflected in his eyes, he made me feel cherished and beautiful. I still remember that night as the moment I was closest to my father.

Why was that moment of comfort so meaningful to me? First, my father was aware of my pain, and he took the time to listen. Providing me a shoulder to cry on was important, but it was not enough. After he listened, he acted. He demonstrated his love for me and showed me how I could grow through disappointment and become stronger.

Our sons and daughters reach out for help countless times. Just as an infant returns to his parents' arms for "emotional refueling," our children continue to need love and support as they venture out on their own. Our homes should be havens of peace where they can feel understood, aided, and encouraged.

But it isn't that simple. Parents have their own problems. They come home weary from their jobs, worried about finances and office conflicts; they may be struggling with inner frustrations, illness, or difficulties in their marriage. In order to help their children become stronger, they have to overcome their own sense of inadequacy.

Parents sometimes suffer from the way they were treated as children: a father batters his son because he was battered as a boy. We are shocked when we read about child abuse. We are indignant. How could a parent strike out at a help-less child? Sometimes the parents are just as bewildered by their sudden outbursts of anger. Such parents, says John White, can be full of rage one moment and express great tenderness the next, "planting a futile kiss on a soft, sleeping cheek."

Child abuse is an extreme example, but it illustrates the complexity of parental love. As a psychiatrist, John White sees parents every day who tell him: "I'd rather hurt myself than harm my children." And yet they continue their deeply ingrained destructive behavior.

In his book *Parents in Pain* (Intervarsity, 1979), White describes the insidious way that a home can become a battleground rather than a refuge. Trust erodes, arguments arise, and parents and children turn against each other, destroying the bonds of affection that hold them together.

Lies can divide families; angry words can wound. A child is suspected of lying. The parent is disappointed and hurt. "I've always taught you to be honest," says the father. He accuses his daughter, who screams back, "I am not lying!" His authority is threatened; he is enraged because he can't penetrate her defenses. She in turn becomes more hostile.

John White suggests that this confrontation might be turned into a helpful conversation if the father talked to his daugher this way: "Lies separate us, Jane. They divide the family. Neither you nor I want to live in a home where neither can trust the other, yet every lie drives us further apart. But every admission of a lie does more than undo a lie. It makes me want to put my arms around you tightly because I know what a price you're paying and how much you want to put things right."

The difference between the two examples is clear. In the first instance, father and daughter become antagonists, locked in a power struggle that neither can win. In the second, father and daughter are partners, working together to solve the problem. Instead of belittling his daughter, the loving father affirms her, offering her sympathy and providing a way for her to deal with her struggle.

Putting things right through reconciliation requires open communication, confession and forgiveness, understanding and compromise. The process often is painful, but without it healing cannot occur.

Christians are commanded to walk in the light, not in the darkness. In order to enjoy an intimate relationship with each other and God our heavenly Father, we need to lead broken, transparent lives, confessing our sins continually. "God is light and in him is no darkness at all . . . if we walk in the light, as he is in the light, we have fellowship with one another, and the blood of Jesus his Son cleanses us from all sin" (1 John 1:5-7).

Brokenness leads to commitment and commitment to community. One of the best ways to strengthen unity in a family and to settle differences is to share in group prayer. "Confess your sins to one another, and pray for one another, that you may be healed" (James 5:16). It is important for our children to realize that before the eyes of God we are all equal. "*All* have sinned" (Rom. 3:23).

We can forgive our children because we have been forgiven. A Christian who has experienced the depths of God's mercy marvels at the Father's infinite kindness and long-suffering and knows how undeserving he is of God's love. "We all are healers who can reach out to offer health," writes Henri Nouwen in *Reaching Out*, "and we all are patients in constant need of help."

As our children see that we rely on our heavenly Father for strength, they also will learn to turn to him in trouble. We may not always be sensitive to their hidden cries; we may not be wise enough to know how to comfort them. But God will never fail them.

As Christians we need to teach our children that God comforts and forgives, but he also chastens us to prevent us from stumbling into sin. "For the Lord disciplines him whom he loves, and chastises every son whom he receives"

(Heb. 12:6). As soon as we come under his lordship, he begins to train us and correct us so that we can learn to control our weaknesses before we harm ourselves and hurt others.

There are times when God chooses to send suffering to a Christian as an act of discipline—in order to prevent greater pain later. As C. S. Lewis pointed out, good can come from suffering if the sufferer learns submission to the will of God. "The father uses his authority to make the son into the sort of human being, he, rightly, and in his superior wisdom, wants him to be," says Lewis. God may allow us to suffer the folly and foolishness of our sin so that we will correct our life and bring it into line with his will for us.

As soon as we are mature enough to correct ourselves, we have no need for correction. Little by little, a child can be taught to control his weaknesses by himself. Sometimes pain provides the opportunity that a parent has been seeking to teach such a lesson. When a child is hurting, he is open and ready to listen.

I was playing outside
When she called me a name
I got mad, I mean really mad,
So I came home and told you,
And you sat down and spoke to me of
Anger, the anger that was suffocating
All the beauty, truth and reason in my life.
At that moment/Anger/Like a fishbone
Stuck coarsely in my throat.
You talked and gave me calm and comfort.
And you taught me a forever lesson.
From you I learned that

Only love removes my anger
In a safe and painless way.

We are made in God's image, meant to mirror his beauty, truth, and reason. Sin blots out that perfect reflection. We can never rub the mirror completely clean by our own efforts. But by the grace of God, one day we will be made perfect. "When the perfect comes, the imperfect will pass away. . . . For now we see in a mirror dimly, but then face to face" (1 Cor. 13:10, 12).

In our struggle against sin, Scripture tells us, we should look to Jesus, "the pioneer and perfecter of our faith" (Heb. 12:2). Christ has gone before us, suffering and conquering all sorrow. To share in our trials, the Son of God came to earth as the Son of man. He suffered pain and persecution; he was hungry, homeless, humiliated, spat upon, and, at the end of his life, deserted by his friends.

Even Jesus had to learn obedience through suffering. On the night of his betrayal, he pleaded with God to spare his life. He fell on his face in such agony that "his sweat was like drops of blood falling to the ground" (Luke 22:44 NIV). Nevertheless, he trusted his Father in faith. "Not my will, but yours be done," said Jesus.

Christ faced his inner struggle alone. He had asked his closest friends to surround him for support. Three times he found them sleeping. Another disciple delivered Jesus to his death with the sign of a kiss. One by one, our Lord suffered the loss of every relationship that was dear to him— even communion with his Father.

"My God, my God, why has thou forsaken me?" Jesus cried out on the cross (Mark 15:34). When Christ took

111

upon himself the sins of the world, he experienced total abandonment and alienation from the Father. At that terrible moment, God turned his back, and the earth was covered with darkness.

Christ's suffering was awful in its magnitude; his loneliness was far more terrifying than anything we will ever have to face. No sorrow is too deep for him to understand. Because Christ shared our pain, our tears move him with compassion. Because he transcended human suffering, he offers us comfort that strengthens and renews.

Christ died as the Son of man, but he rose again as the Son of God. The darkness of Calvary was followed by a bursting forth of light as Christ ascended to glory. As children of God, we will all share in that glory.

What will we see when we stand face to face with our heavenly Father? Pure light. "And night shall be no more," John says, describing heaven, ". . . the Lord God will be their light" (Rev. 22:5). Without the darkness of sin, Christians are promised there will be no more death or sorrow or crying or pain. God himself will wipe away every tear.

And, Paul adds, we will be completely one with God. "Now I know in part; then I shall understand fully, even as I have been fully understood" (1 Cor. 13:12). Just as a newborn rests in his mother's arms, in a heavenly dialogue of merging, body-molding unity, we will once again experience that perfect peace and wholeness in God's presence.

In our earthly life God reaches out to us with compassion and comfort. We can help our own children in the same way. We cry with them because we have suffered too. We offer them hope because we know that pain is only temporary and sometimes is necessary for growth. From a Christian perspective we can assure them that all suffering will one day pass away.

And so, the ugly duckling flies away as a swan and the tears of childbirth give way to a song: "Weeping may endure for a night, but joy cometh in the morning" (Ps. 30:5 KJV).

9

A Time to Let Go

Loosening the ties
of parenthood

When she was tiny, Brenna used to lie content and calm on Larry's chest, soaking up his body heat for comfort. Now she shoots out of his arms like a bar of soap, always on the move, eager to explore her ever-widening world. She is changing fast, propelling herself beyond our embrace and beyond our control.

"I wish I could freeze her," says Larry wistfully. Of course if he did stop Brenna's perpetual motion, she would merely be a toy to gratify his pleasure, an object with no life of her own. And he knows that each stage in her development brings new joys. He will forfeit those blessings if he clings stubbornly to what she is now. Still, no parent wants to let go.

Am I any better? I try to capture her every antic and facial expression with my camera. "For her grandparents," I tell myself. "To show their friends." And this book. Why am I writing a book about my daughter? To understand her better, to understand my new role as a mother. Yes, but what else? To hold her and never let her go.

I never dared admit that until I heard another mother say those words. One evening we went with friends to the airport to receive their adopted daughter from India. Sasha had flown 33 hours with four escorts, and Marta had been warned that her new daughter might reject her. But as soon as she saw Marta, the little girl with soft, dark skin and large, peaceful eyes melted into her arms. "I felt an overwhelming sense of joy," said Marta, with tears in her eyes. "I wanted to hold her and never let her go."

It is difficult to describe the mystery and ecstasy of that first embrace. The glow of that meeting always remains new and untarnished in the minds of parents, despite the frustrating and demanding days that follow. In that moment, they give their hearts completely to their baby.

No relationship is so intense as the love between parent and child, and none is so dynamic. It is always changing. The same natural forces that draw parent and infant together into mutual dependence will also drive them apart. Inherent in oneness are the seeds of separateness.

This, says Edith Neisser, is the paradox of parenthood. In *Mothers and Daughters* (Harper & Row, 1973) she writes: "It is hard to realize the moment a daughter is born, when the link with her is strong and the pleasure and problems involved in the shaping of ties to her lie ahead, that eventually reshaping and gradually loosening those ties will also be a part of parenthood."

In order for Larry and me to relinquish our ties to Brenna gradually, we need to remind ourselves that letting go is not a series of traumas that we will have to face in the future: sending her to school, seeing her off to college, giving her away in marriage. It is a continual process that begins at the day of birth.

Brenna is a constant reminder of this herself. The impulses that compel a child to separate from his parents are inborn and necessary for growth. As soon as Brenna's eyes focused on my face, her gaze began to wander to the world beyond. She reached out, crawled away, and stood one day tottering on uncertain legs.

An infant cannot stop his drive to expand his horizons any more than his parents can. He is often frightened and perplexed by his longing to remain one with his mother and his urge to launch out on his own. This tension between oneness and separateness reaches its peak at a year and a half when an infant truly becomes an individual.

The emergence of selfhood, which occurs between 18 months and three years, is called the second birth. There are similarities between this psychological birth and physical birth. As the ebb and flow of contractions work together to push a baby out into the world, so the toddler moves toward and away from his mother, pushing himself out of her embrace.

There are also vital differences between the first and second birth. "Whereas physical birth meant a rupturing of the bonds," writes Louise Kaplan, "psychological birth strengthens the bonds of love and attachment between a child and his parents." The infant is transformed from an unthinking, irresponsible newborn who reacts purely by instincts and reflexes to a self-aware individual capable of thought and self-determination. Now he offers his parents love because he chooses to, not because he has to out of dependence or to gratify his needs.

In the second birth, the child himself does all the birth work. His parents can offer empathy and comfort, but they

116

cannot do the work for him. The best way they can help is to understand the crisis that the self-aware toddler is going through.

A child's dawning sense of self can be threatening and trying if parents are unprepared. With the onset of the "terrible twos" I was told to expect the worst: temper tantrums, a ceaseless battle of wills, and explosions of "no" and "mine." I should have been told that a toddler's no-saying leads to his saying yes.

No-saying helps a child define the distance between himself and his parents. As the toddler becomes aware that he is not merely an extension of his parents, he has to establish his own separate identity. He does this by testing his parents and himself.

At first the toddler's no is simply an echo of Mom and Dad's. Mimicking us, Brenna began to furrow her brow and bat the air with her hands, shouting "No!" She repeated the word over and over again, studying the nuances of the sound and posturing her body for effect. Her noes became more emphatic: "Nnnnno!"

No was not just another word: it was a command invested with power. Soon Brenna's noes were directed at us. She looked us straight in the eye when she said them, throwing out her arms with great bravado as if she were conducting an orchestra. Actually that's exactly what she was trying to do—conduct her own life.

And we were out of tune. The inner harmony of merging oneness had been shattered by discord. Brenna's wishes did not always coincide with ours. When she wanted to stay up at night and roughhouse with Daddy, we sent her to bed. When she wanted to dig dirt out of the plant pot and smear it on the living room rug, Mommy insisted that the dirt should stay in the pot.

Sometimes she became exasperated with us and marched into the bathroom, slamming the door behind her. By physical separation she was announcing her emotional distance from us. After a few minutes she would reappear, content and happy, ready to be friends again.

A toddler's growing independence isn't always expressed in defiant showdowns and tantrums. It can be playful. I called Brenna's name one afternoon, expecting her to run to me. She didn't answer. I called again and again. Still no answer. Suddenly I panicked, checking in all the rooms, looking in closets and under beds. Finally I found her huddled under the dining room table, quiet as a mouse. "Brenna, you scared Mommy!" She smiled slyly with an air of triumph. She had made *me* run to her.

After this happened several times, I realized that her hide-and-seek games were experiments with separateness just as peek-a-boo had been when she was an infant. I had initiated the game then; now she took the lead and I followed.

There were other times when Brenna's bravado left her. She would curl up in a corner and suck her thumb looking dejected and downcast. One moment she was flying high, exhilarated with her independence, then just as quickly she would come crashing to the ground, somber and sad.

As Brenna acted out the drama between oneness and separateness, she became more capricious and unpredictable, swinging erratically from one mood to another. This was particularly evident in her relationship with me. She would shadow my every move, hovering at my heels, clinging to my clothes. When her father came home, she darted away and clung to him, coyly rejecting me. Kaplan calls this pattern of shadowing and darting away, holding on and letting go, the "tempestuous choreography."

It is awesome for an infant suddenly to realize that he is

alone. Overnight it seems his world is turned upside down. He can't go back to the simple days when he was protected and enveloped by an all-good mothering presence. Now he is frightened of being swallowed up by his mother, but he is equally afraid of losing her love. He discovers that she isn't perfect; she can disappoint him and make him mad. And he recognizes that he isn't perfect either. His actions anger her. They even anger and confuse him.

Out of this tempest eventually comes calm. Another kind of wholeness is achieved between parent and child. "This second source of personal wholeness is more complex than the first," writes Kaplan, "because it includes all the varied emotions, thoughts, fantasies and values that are involved when we relate to down-to-earth, in-the-flesh actual persons." Parent and child begin to relate to one another as individuals.

When I lock eyes with my new, self-aware daughter, we no longer passively merge into a blissful state of oneness. Her looks are questioning, challenging, sometimes defiant. Now there is a creative tension and active rhythm to our dialogue. We have learned to appreciate each other's separateness and are both enriched by it.

As parents, it is easy to be so preoccupied with our own struggle to let go that we forget our children are struggling too. The crisis of the second birth is only the beginning of a child's journey into selfhood. Every time his "growth urges" push him beyond himself into the unknown, he is thrown into limbo again, uncertain of who he is and what he will become.

A toddler's tantrums and a teenager's rebellion spring from fear. Underneath the violence and anger the child is asking his parents, "Do you still love me?" He also wonders, "Will I still love myself if I become a different person?" With each growth spurt, the child has to come to terms with a new self.

Because his world is always changing, he needs to know that some things never change, especially his parents' love.

In the parable of the prodigal son, the loving father let his son leave home though he knew that the boy was not ready for complete independence. When he returned home, contrite and defeated, his father welcomed him with open arms. He could have lectured the boy or said, "I told you so," but he didn't. With great rejoicing, said Jesus, the father threw his arms around his son and kissed him.

Did the father know his son would return? I think he probably did. He knew that he had to let his son go to allow him to grow and change and find his own way. He could not live his son's life for him.

Left to wander alone, the young boy became hopelessly lost and confused. Only one thing was certain in his life— his father's love. It shown like a beacon in the darkness, reminding him of the safe, protected harbor of home. It also reminded him of the best in himself and the steady course that his father hoped he would follow.

"Train up a child in the way he should go," Solomon advised, "and when he is old he will not depart from it" (Prov. 22:6). We do not own our children. They belong to the heavenly Father; he entrusts them to us temporarily for training. Our job as Christian parents is to help our sons and daughters discover their unique paths in life and become the men and women God intends them to be.

Charles Swindoll, in his book *You and Your Child* (Thomas Nelson, 1977) points out that the word *way* in Proverbs 22:6 is the same Hebrew word used in the Psalms to describe the *bending* of a bow before an arrow flies to a target. "In every child God places in our arms," says Swindoll, "there is a *bent*, a set of characteristics already established. The bent is fixed and determined before he is given over to

121

our care." If we raise our children in keeping with their true nature or individual bent, they will continue to go God's way even after they outgrow their need for our support and guidance.

As our children mature and take charge of their own lives, our relationship to them changes. They no longer regard us as super beings, all-powerful and wise. They come to realize that we are flawed, imperfect people just as they are. It suddenly occurs to them that we don't have all the answers. We are searching too.

As Christian parents, we should not be ashamed to admit that to our children. The spiritual journey is dynamic and ever-changing, always challenging us to better ourselves. Christians can never achieve the perfection that Christ calls us to, but that is the adventure of faith. The alternative is looking at life as static, unchanging, leading nowhere. Christianity is an open road, not a dead end.

It is thrilling to imagine, as I watch my daughter's psychological journey from infanthood to self-awareness, that someday she will embark on a spiritual quest to discover a fuller, deeper knowledge of herself. The same God who gave her an inborn urge to reach out and develop her human potential also endowed her with a thirst for spiritual awareness. Without that dimension she can never know herself completely.

Just as Brenna's psychological journey is characterized by a back and forth movement between oneness and separateness, her spiritual pilgrimage will evolve in the same way—with a back and forth movement toward God.

In the beginning, there will be the ecstasy of the embrace when she discovers God's special love for her. As she gazes into her heavenly Father's eyes, she will see herself from his point of view, a newborn with boundless potential. "A baby gets to know what he is by what is mirrored in the faces

122

of those who look at him," says Louise Kaplan. In his parents eyes he sees "all the spectacular and powerful things he sometimes imagines himself to be."

The love that Brenna sees reflected in our eyes is only a fraction of the immeasurable adoration that the heavenly Father feels for her. God is a doting parent; each of his children is precious and supremely valued. "He encircled him, he cared for him," says Moses, describing God's tender love for Israel, "he kept him as the apple of his eye" (Deut. 32:10).

But the heavenly Father does not demand mechanical devotion. We are not objects created to gratify his pleasure. We are living beings with minds and wills of our own. As persons who reflect the attributes of a personal God, we have the dignity of choice and self-determination. We can choose God's way, or we can choose to go our own way.

When Brenna yearns for independence and chooses to venture beyond the boundaries of God's care and protection, he will let her go. Like the father of the prodigal son, he gives her that freedom even though he is fully aware of the danger and difficulties she will face.

There will be times when Brenna's life is comfortable and going well. She may lose sight of God and drift away. Suddenly illness or a shattered dream may drive her back to the Father's arms for strength. There may be periods of rebellion or doubt when she rejects God and then embraces him again. The spiritual journey is a series of new beginnings, of turning away from God and turning back to him, of separations and reunions.

Loving parents give their children enough rein to grow and change and become individuals. "God wants us to become persons," says Paul Tournier in *Secrets* (John Knox, 1965). "That is why he respects our revolts, our reticences, our disobediences which alone confer a genuineness on our returns, our confessions, our adoration. . . . He who has never said 'no' to God cannot genuinely say 'yes' to him."

To discover how much we need God, sometimes we have to experience what life is like without him. God allows us to make our own mistakes, to wander where we will and to return to his loving arms, not because we have to but because we want to.

God does not expect us to remain spiritual infants, as "babes in Christ" fed only on milk. He challenges and tests us, and he encourages us to challenge and test him, thereby growing strong on the substantive food of faith. He longs to have an interpersonal relationship with us as responsible, free-thinking individuals. "Thus the Lord used to speak to Moses face to face, as a man speaks to his friend" (Exod. 33:11).

As Brenna matures spiritually, her dialogue with God will become more active and vital, compelling her to a deeper commitment. The heavenly Father will reveal more of his wisdom and understanding to her, enabling her to see more clearly his purpose for her and the role she is meant to play in his plan for others.

Walking with God and sharing his counsel enlarges our horizons. We begin to realize that our lives are bound up with others; that God's direction for us is part of a much bigger plan.

A Christian's highest calling is to become a partner in God's divine plan. As Christian parents, Larry and I have the privilege of raising our daughter according to God's purpose and plan for her. It is a labor of love that began before Brenna was born.

God created our little girl. Even before we had given her a name, he knew her intimately. "Thou didst knit me together in my mother's womb," sang the psalmist. "When I was being made in secret, intricately wrought in the depths of the earth, thy eyes beheld my unformed substance" (Ps. 139:13, 15-16).

As Larry and I held Brenna in our arms, we wondered what kind of person she would be and what she would become. We looked at her with eyes of love and wanted the very best for her; we dreamed big dreams. While we were dreaming, our heavenly Father, the Parent of us all, had already charted a course for her life. "In thy book were written, every one of them, the days that were formed for me, when as yet there was none of them" (Ps. 139:16).

God's vision for Brenna is broader and more far-reaching than anything we can ever imagine. In his perfect wisdom, he knows what is most beneficial for her; in his perfect love, he desires her deepest happiness.

As we give our daughter up to the Lord, we don't know what the future will bring. The direction of Brenna's life is still a mystery to us. Little by little, step by step, it will be revealed. Our task is simply to set her going God's way.

The profoundest thing
one can say of a river
is that it's on its way to the sea.

The deepest thought
one can think of a person
is that he or she is a citizen of eternity.

Moments and years,
years and moments,
pass like sea-bent streams.
And I? I'm carried by the current

of an all-possessing Love.
I'm on my way, God's way for me,
so let it be.

Gerhard E. Frost, "His Way for Me"

When Brenna was two months old, we entrusted her to God's keeping and the care of his people. As a symbol of this commitment, the pastor took Brenna in his arms and walked up and down the aisle, presenting her to the congregation.

"This child is now received into the church of Jesus Christ," he said. "See what love the Father has given us, that we should be called children of God."

One of the greatest gifts the Lord has given us is each other. "God setteth the solitary in families" (Ps. 68:6 KJV). Brenna is not only a member of our family; she also belongs to the church, God's extended family.

As a member of that caring community, she will never journey alone. In her spiritual quest, she will always be surrounded by people who share a common purpose. In their midst she will learn to give and receive love, to serve and be served, and to lay down her life for her friends. Through loving and serving and sacrificing, she will discover God's way for her and be part of the eternal current of love that flows from generation to generation. So let it be.

Acknowledgments

Lyrics from "I Am a Rock" on page 10 are © 1965 Paul Simon. Used by permission.

The passage by Gibran on page 13 is reprinted from *The Prophet*, by Kahlil Gibran, by permission of Alfred A. Knopf, Inc. Copyright 1923 by Kahlil Gibran and renewed 1951 by Administrators C.T.A. of Kahlil Gibran Estate, and Mary G. Gibran.

Concepts on pages 52-54 are taken from *A Shepherd Looks at Psalm 23* by W. Phillip Keller. Copyright © 1970 by W. Phillip Keller. Used by permission of Zondervan Publishing House.

The quotation from a Charlie Brown cartoon on page 58 is from *Security Is a Thumb and a Blanket,* by Charles M. Schulz, © 1963 by United Feature Syndicate, Inc., published by Determined Productions, San Francisco.

The excerpt from *The Velveteen Rabbit* by Margery Williams on pages 70-71 is reprinted by permission of Doubleday & Company, Inc. and William Heinemann Ltd.

The poem "Antidote to Anger" on pages 110-111 is reprinted from *Marriage Encounter,* June 1981. Volume 10, Number 6. Used with permission of publisher.

The poem "His Way for Me" on pages 125-126 is from *Blessed Is the Ordinary* by Gerhard E. Frost. Copyright © 1980 Gerhard E. Frost. Published by Winston Press, Inc., 430 Oak Grove, Minneapolis, MN 55403. All rights reserved. Used with permission.